WILLIAM ✠ KU-612-850

Prayers for
Young People

Collins
FONTANA BOOKS

First published by Wm Collins Sons & Co Ltd 1963
First issued in Fontana Books 1966
Fourteenth Impression October 1975

© William Barclay 1963
Printed in Great Britain
Collins Clear-Type Press
London and Glasgow

For Fiona

You and Your Prayers

Prayer is like any other great and valuable gift or possession—we will never get the best and the most from it, unless we learn to use it aright. This means that there are certain things which we must always bear in mind when we pray.

i. The very first thing that we must remember is that God wants us to pray to him. There are times when people make it quite clear that we are a nuisance to them, and when quite clearly they cannot be bothered with us. No one is ever a nuisance to God. Once when Jesus talked to God, he used a word to address God which to us is a foreign word. He called God, 'Abba, Father' (Mark 14:36). Afterwards Paul said that this word Abba is the word that any Christian can use when he talks to God (Romans 8:15). It is just not possible to translate this word Abba into English. It was the word which a young child used in Palestine in the time of Jesus when he talked to his father, just as to this day Arab boys and girls call their father *iaba*. It is really the eastern word for Daddy. This means that we can talk to God just as easily and just as simply as we talk to our own father in our own home.

Once someone asked a wise man how to set about praying. The wise man said: 'Just take a chair and put it opposite you, and think to yourself that God is sitting on that chair, and just talk to him in the way that you would talk to your closest friend.'

Prayer should not be unnatural and difficult; it should

7

be as natural and as easy as talking to the person you know and love best of all.

In prayer we do not need any special words or any special language. We do not need to say 'thou' and 'thee'. That is the way the Bible has it, because that is the way in which people used ordinarily to talk long ago. We can use to God the same kind of language as we use every day. We do not need to be in any special place to pray. We can pray anywhere. Of course, it is easier to pray in some places than it is in others. In a church or in a great cathedral we cannot help having a feeling of reverence. But God is just as near us in a room in our own home, on the street, in a class-room, on a playing-field, on a hill-top, as he is in any church or in any cathedral. We do not need to be in any special position to pray to God. We can pray walking along the road, sitting in a chair, standing on a moor or by the sea-shore, even lying in bed, just as well as we can pray kneeling. When we pray, all we have got to do is just to speak to God as we speak to our best friend.

ii. When we pray we have to remember that we do not need to squeeze things out of God, as if he had to be persuaded into giving them to us. God wants to give us his good gifts even more than we want to ask him for them. Sometimes when we want something from a human person, we have to pester him into giving it to us; we have to break down his resistance. But God is not like that. He is more eager to give than we are to ask.

iii. Of course, that does not mean that, if we want something, we have only to ask for it. It is very important to remember that God knows what is good for us far better than we know ourselves; and there are times when we pray for things which in the end would not be for our good. When we were very young we often wanted to do things like playing with matches; or we often wanted far more sweets or fruit than was good for us; or we wanted to do something which more experienced people knew could only lead to trouble. When that kind of thing happened, those who loved us had to refuse to give us what we wanted. Sometimes God has to do that. It is not that God does not answer our prayers; it is that God answers them, not in our way, but in his.

There is a problem here. If God knows everything, if God knows what is good for us better than we know ourselves, why bother to pray at all? If God knows it all, what need is there for us to speak to him? We talk about God knowing our secret thoughts; if we go to Church at all, we must have heard the prayer which begins: 'Almighty God, unto whom all hearts be open, all desires known, and from whom no secrets are hid'; if this is so, what is the sense in praying to one who knows what we want to pray for before we pray for it?

This is something about which we must think, for we certainly will not ever really pray, if we think in our heart of hearts that prayer is really a waste of time. Let us think about this in relation to the five different kinds of prayer.

There is the prayer which we call *invocation*. Invocation literally means a calling in. In the prayer of invocation we ask for God's presence with us, or, to put it better, because God is always with us, we ask God to make us aware that he is with us. Now, one of the great stories of Jesus after his resurrection tells how he met in with two people who were on the road from Jerusalem to Emmaus. They did not recognize him, but they were thrilled and fascinated by the things which he told them. They came near to the village and to the house where these two people lived. And then it says of Jesus: 'He made as though he would have gone further.' But they begged him to come into their house and visit them, and so he

9

did (Luke 24:28,29). There is about God and Jesus what we can only call a very wonderful courtesy. We cannot go into someone else's house without an invitation. It would be very impolite and very discourteous to burst in all uninvited; we wait until we are asked. God is like that. God wants to come into our life; he wants to meet us; but he waits until we ask him to come in to us. Of course, God shows us in all kinds of ways that he wants us to know him and to love him and to talk to him; but, like a courteous guest, he waits until we invite him in just as Jesus did on the road to Emmaus long ago. That is the first reason why we must speak to him, although he knows it all already.

There is the prayer which we call *confession*. Confession means telling God about the wrong things that we have done, saying that we are sorry for them, and asking him to forgive us for them. We know what happens at home. We do something wrong, and then we regret it. We know quite well that our parents really know that we are sorry, and we know quite well that they will forgive us. But between us and them there is a kind of invisible barrier, there is the feeling that something is wrong, there is a kind of atmosphere of unhappiness and strangeness, until we go to them and say: 'I'm sorry I was bad; I'll try not to do it again.' And immediately we have gone to them and said it, things are all right again. It is just the same with us and God. We know that nothing that we can do will stop God loving us; we know that he is always willing to forgive us; but things are not right between us and him until we go to him and say that we are sorry for what we have done.

There is the prayer which we call *thanksgiving*. Thanksgiving means thanking God for all the good gifts which he has given to us. One of the great dangers of life is that we should take things for granted just because they come to us regularly and every day. And it is never enough just to feel grateful to those who are kind to us; we must sometimes express our gratitude in words. A great many people have had an experience like this. They have known when they were young that their parents were very good and very kind to them, but they never said thank you and never said how grateful they were. Then the day came when their parents died, and when they looked back, they were forced to say to themselves: 'I wish I had told my father and mother how grateful I was for all that they did for me.' It is only courteous and polite to say thanks when people are kind to us. It is just the same with God. It is an ugly thing to take everything as a matter of course and never to say a word of thanks.

There is the prayer which we call *petition*. Petition means asking God for the things which we know we need, not only the material things, but the qualities of mind and heart and character which will enable us to live well and to make something out of life. But, if God knows what we need even better than we do, and if God knows what is good for us better than we know ourselves, why ask him for anything? It often happens in life that an older and a wiser person knows very well that something would be good for a younger person; but he does not know whether the younger person would accept it, if he offered it, and sometimes he even knows that the younger person would refuse to accept it. Often God cannot give us the things we need until we are prepared to consent to take them; and petition means asking God to give us the things which he knows we need, and telling him that we are ready now to take them. In fact, the best kind of petition is to tell God what we want, and then to say to him: 'Lord, give me not what I want, but what you know I need. Your will be done.' Often a teacher knows that a boy would make a first-class scholar, but he cannot give him the extra teaching and the extra work and the extra study, unless the boy will accept them. Often a trainer knows that a boy would make a first-class athlete, but he cannot give him the extra training and discipline until the boy is willing to accept them. God knows what is best for us, but God cannot give it to us, until we tell him that we are ready to take it. That is why we must tell God that we are ready and willing to accept his gifts.

The last kind of prayer is the prayer which we call *intercession*. Intercession means praying for other people. It is very natural to pray for people when we love them and when we want the best for them. All men and women and boys and girls are children of God. If you want really to please a parent, and really to make a parent happy, then the surest way to do it is to do something for the parent's son or daughter. And it pleases God most of all when he knows that we love and care for others who are his children. That is why it brings special pleasure to God when we pray for others.

When we come to think of it, we can see quite clearly that, although God does know it all already, there is every reason for telling him about it in our prayers.

iv. There is another thing which we must remember about prayer, and it is one of the most important things of all. We must never look on prayer as the easy way out, as the way to get things done without any effort and trouble and labour on our part. God will never do for us what we can do for ourselves, and, when we pray, we must immediately do all we can to make our own prayers come true. It would be no good at all to pray to God to make us good at our lessons and successful in our examinations, unless we work and study as hard as we can. It would be quite useless to pray to God to make us good at athletics, unless we train as strenuously as we can. If we are ill, it would be no good to pray to God to make us well again, unless we obey the doctor, observe the diet that is set down for us, and take the medicine which is prescribed for us. It would, for instance, be quite useless for a person with a stomach ulcer to pray to God for health, and then to continue living on a diet of fried food. Prayer is not God doing things for us; prayer is God helping us to do things for ourselves.

Someone has said that God has four answers to prayer. Sometimes he says, Yes. Sometimes he says, No. Sometimes he says, Wait. Most of all he says, If. He says: 'I will help you, *if* you will do everything you can to help yourself.'

It is the same when we pray for other people. It is no good asking God to help the poor people, or to cheer the lonely people, unless we are prepared to give something to help those who are poor, and to visit those who are lonely.

Prayer is not an excuse for being lazy and for pushing all the work off on to God; prayer is a way to finding the strength and ability to do things along with God that we could never have done by ourselves.

v. There is another way of putting this. Prayer is not usually escape from things; prayer is the way to find strength to bear and to overcome things. Prayer will not cure a condition, for instance, which requires an operation to make us well again; but prayer will make us able to be cheerful and calm so that we will get well all the sooner. Suppose we plan to do something on a certain day, and suppose we want the sun to shine, it is no good praying that it will not rain. Whether it rains or not depends on the natural laws on which this world is founded. What we can and ought to do is to pray that, hail, rain or shine, we will be able to enjoy ourselves. It is no good praying that we should win a race or a game;

what we can do is to pray that, win or lose, we should play fair, and that we should take victory or defeat in the right spirit. Prayer does not usually stop things happening; it enables us to bear them and to conquer them when they do happen. Prayer is not a way of running away from things; it is a way of meeting them and beating them.

vi. There is one more thing left to say. Up to this point we have been thinking of prayer as if it were always we who were talking to God; but prayer is not only talking to God; prayer is just as much listening to God. Prayer is not only us telling God what we want; it is God telling us what he wants. It is not only us saying to God 'Lord, I want you to do this for me'; it is us saying to God: 'Lord, what do you want me to do?' That must mean that in all our prayers there must be a time when we stop speaking and when we listen in silence for what God wants to say to us. In prayer we must never be so busy talking that we never listen, and we must never speak so much that we give God no chance to speak. Remember in prayer always to have a silence when we listen to God.

There are very many people who only pray when they are in trouble and when things go wrong. But it is a poor kind of person who only goes to visit a friend when he wants something out of him. We ought to pray every day in life, for we need God all the time. We ought to pray before we go out in the morning. Maybe we will not have much time in the morning but we can at least pray the prayer that old Sir Jacob Astley prayed before the Battle of Edgehill: 'O Lord, thou knowest how busy I must be this day; if I forget thee, do not thou forget me.' And we ought always to pray before we go to sleep at night. It will make a difference if we begin and continue and end every day with God.

You and Your Prayers

This book is meant to help you to pray. There is in it a morning and evening prayer for each week for a year. Sometimes people do not pray because they do not really know what to say and how to put it. This book is meant to help you every morning and every evening to have a minute or two with God. But I hope that this book will be only a start for you, and that very soon the day will come when you will not need this book to help you to pray any more, but when you can talk to God, not in the words of this book, but in your own words, as easily as you talk to your best friend.

William Barclay

PRAYERS FOR YOUNG PEOPLE

MORNING

O God, my Father, thank you for last night's sleep and
thank you for today.

Help me to waste none of today's hours and to miss none
of today's opportunities.

Help me all through today always to obey my conscience
and always to do what I know is right, so that I may
do nothing for which I would be sorry and ashamed
at the end of the day.

Help me so to live today that at the end of the day I may
be tired but happy, with nothing to regret.

This I ask for Jesus' sake. Amen.

EVENING

Forgive me, O God, for anyone whom I have hurt, or
failed, or disappointed today, and for any wrong thing
I have said or done today.

Thank you for all the new things I have learned today
and for all the things I have enjoyed today.

Give me a good night's sleep tonight, and grant that
tomorrow morning I may waken refreshed for work
and for play.

This I ask for Jesus' sake. Amen

MORNING

Make me all through today, O God,
Obedient to my parents;
Respectful to my teachers;
Diligent in my work;
Fair in my games;
Clean in my pleasure;
Kind to those whom I can help;
True to my friends;
And loyal to you.
This I ask for Jesus' sake. Amen.

EVENING

O God, bless those who are not so fortunate as I am.

Bless those whose homes are unhappy and whose parents are unkind.

Bless those who are ill. Specially bless those who are away from home in hospitals and in infirmaries and who are feeling everything very strange and who are a little afraid.

Bless those who are poor and hungry and cold.

Grant that in my happiness I may not forget the needs of others.

This I ask for Jesus' sake. Amen.

MORNING

O God, thank you for making me as I am.
Thank you for health and strength;
> For eyes to see;
> For ears to hear;
> For hands to work;
> For feet to walk and run;
> For a mind to think;
> For a memory to remember;
> For a heart to love.
Thank you for
> Parents who are kind to me;
> Friends who are true to me;
> Teachers who are patient with me.
Thank you for this wonderful life. Help me to try to deserve all your gifts a little more.
This I ask for Jesus' sake. Amen.

EVENING

Thank you, O God, for everything that has happened today, and thank you for bringing me safely to the end of today.
Forgive me for anything I said or did today for which now I am ashamed.
Forgive me,
> If I have worried my parents;
> If I have disappointed my friends;
> If I have caused trouble to my teachers;
> If I have let myself down.
Tomorrow is another day. Please help me to do better in it.
This I ask for Jesus' sake. Amen.

MORNING

O God, help me to cure my faults.
Keep me from being
Cheeky in my conversation;
Sulky when I get a row which I deserve;
Lazy at my lessons;
Disobliging at home;
Too conceited when I do well;
Too discouraged when I fail.
Help me to walk looking to Jesus, and always to try to
be more like him.
This I ask for his sake. Amen.

EVENING

Thank you, O God, for all the people with whom I have
learned lessons, played games, and walked and talked
today.
Thank you for all the people who have been kind to
me today:
For those whose work and whose love give me the
things I need, the food I eat, the clothes I wear,
the comfort I enjoy;
For those who have taught me the things which I
must know, if I am to do a man's job in the world
when I grow up;
For those who are a fine example to me of how I
ought to live;
For friends without whom life could never be the
same.
Thank you most of all for Jesus, my Master, my Example,
my Friend.
Help me to sleep well tonight and to live well tomorrow.
This I ask for Jesus' sake. Amen.

MORNING

O Lord Jesus, be with me all through today to help me
to live as I ought to live.

Be with me at my lessons,
so that I may never give up any task, no matter how
hard and difficult it is, until I have mastered it, and so
that I will not allow anything to beat me.

Be with me at my games,
so that, whether I win or lose, I may play fair, and so
that if I win I may not boast, and if I lose I may not
make excuses.

Be with me in my pleasure,
so that I may never find pleasure in anything that I
would afterwards regret, or in anything that I would
not like you or my parents to see me do.

Be with me in my home,
so that I may be kind and considerate, and that I may
try to make the work of others easier and not harder.

Be with me in the streets,
so that I may be a credit to my school and to my
uniform and to those who love me and to myself.

Help me to be the kind of boy you want me to be.

This I ask for your love's sake. Amen.

EVENING

Forgive me, O God,

> If today there has been on my lips any word that was bad or untrue;
>
> If today there has been in my mind any thought that was envious or jealous or impure;
>
> If today I have listened to things which I should have refused to listen to;
>
> If today at any time I have been ashamed to show that I belong to you.

Help me to remember that you are always with me, so that I will always speak the truth, and do the right, and be afraid of nothing.

This I ask for Jesus' sake. Amen.

MORNING

O God, all through today help me,

> Not to lose my temper even when people and things annoy me;
>
> Not to lose my patience even when things do not come out right the first time;
>
> Not to lose my hope when things are difficult and when learning is hard;
>
> Not to lose my goodness and my honour, even when I am tempted to take the wrong way.

Help me so to live today that I will have nothing to be sorry for when I go to bed again at night.

Hear this my prayer for Jesus' sake. Amen.

EVENING

O God, forgive me for anything that I have done today which I would not want my parents to know about and which I would not want you to see.

Forgive me for anything in today which I could have done very much better than I did it.

Forgive me for wasting my time, and for spending my time on the wrong things.

Forgive me for everything for which I am sorry now; and help me to sleep well tonight, and to do better tomorrow.

This I ask for Jesus' sake. Amen.

Second Month: Second Week

Help me today, O God,
    At school to concentrate on my work, and not to let
        my thoughts wander;
    At games to play hard and to play fair;
    At home to do my share in the work without grum-
        bling and without having to be asked twice;
    In my leisure time to enjoy myself in such a way that
        I will do good to myself and no harm to others.
Help me to make this a happy day for myself and for all
    whom I meet.
This I ask for Jesus' sake. Amen.

EVENING

O God, bless those who have to work while I sleep:
    Those who work on the night shift in the works and
        factories and the shipyards and the mines;
    Those who go on journeys on the roads and the
        railways, by sea and in the air, to bring us our
        letters, our newspapers, our food in the morning;
    Police and watchmen who through the night protect
        the public peace and safety;
    Doctors and nurses and all who through the night
        must care for those who are ill and in pain.
Help me to remember all those whose work keeps the
    world and its affairs going, while I sleep.
I know that you never slumber or sleep, and that your
    care for me and your watch over me are unsleeping and
    unceasing. Help me to sleep without fear, and to
    waken refreshed tomorrow.
This I ask for the sake of Jesus, my Lord. Amen.

MORNING

O God, all through today keep me
>   From girning and sulking when I do not get my
>   own way;
>   From being envious and jealous of others who have
>   what I have not got;
>   From doing things with a grumble and a grudge
>   when I am asked to help;
>   From making a nuisance of myself by being obstinate
>   and bad-tempered and disobliging.

All through today help me to make the best of everything
that happens, and to do with all my might whatever
my hand finds to do.

This I ask through Jesus Christ my Lord. Amen.

EVENING

O God, bless the people to whom I owe so much and
without whom my life could never be the same.

Bless my father and mother, and help me to try to show
them that I do love them and that I am grateful to
them.

Bless my brothers and sisters, and don't let there be any
fights and squabbles in this family.

Bless my friends, and keep me true to them and them
true to me.

Bless those who teach me, and help me to be a credit to
them.

Bless me. Forgive me for anything wrong I did or said
or though' today, and help me to do better tomorrow.

This I ask for Jesus' sake. Amen.

Second Month: Fourth Week

O God, help me at my examination today to remember
the things which I have learned and studied.

Help me to remember well and to think clearly.

Help me not to be so nervous and excited that I will not
do myself justice, and keep me calm and clear-headed.

Help me to try my hardest and to do my best.

This I ask for your love's sake. Amen.

EVENING

O God, I know quite well that I bring most of my
troubles on myself.

> I leave things until the last minute, and then I have
> to do them in far too big a hurry to do them
> properly, and so I often come to school with
> lessons half-learned and work half-done.
>
> I don't spend all the time I ought to spend in work
> and in study, although I always mean to.
>
> I get angry and impatient far too easily, and the
> result is that I upset myself and everyone else.
>
> I do things without thinking first, and then I am
> sorry I did them.
>
> I hurt the people I love most of all, and then—too
> late—I am sorry for what I said or did.

It is not that I don't know what is right. I do know—
but the trouble is that I mean to do it and then don't
do it. I need your help to strengthen me and to change
me.

Please help me to do what I cannot do and to be what
I cannot be by myself.

This I ask for your love's sake. Amen.

MORNING

Today, O God, make me
> Brave enough to face the things of which I am afraid;
> Strong enough to overcome the temptations which try to make me do the wrong thing and not to do the right thing;
> Persevering enough to finish every task that is given me to do;
> Kind enough always to be ready to help others;
> Obedient enough to obey your voice whenever you speak to me through my conscience.

Help me
> To live in purity;
> To speak in truth;
> To act in love
>> All through today.

This I ask for Jesus' sake. Amen.

EVENING

O God, thank you for all the things and the people which
make such a difference to my life.

Thank you for

My parents and for all that they give me and all that
they do for me;

My home and for all the happiness and the comfort
which are always waiting there for me;

My friends in whose company I am happy;

My school and for everything I learn there to make
me able some day to earn my own living and to
live my own life;

Jesus to be my Master, my Example, and my best
and truest Friend.

Help me to try to deserve a little better all the wonderful
things which life and you have given to me.

This I ask for your love's sake. Amen.

MORNING

O God, help me to use today as you would wish me to use it.

Don't let me waste my time today. Help me always to know what I ought to be doing, and to do it.

Don't let me miss my opportunities today—opportunities to learn something new, opportunities to help someone in difficulty, opportunities to show those who love me that I love them, opportunities to make myself a little better and a little wiser than I am.

Don't let me quarrel with anyone today; no matter what happens, help me to keep my temper.

Don't let me let myself down today, and don't let me hurt or disappoint those who love me.

All through today don't let me forget Jesus, so that all through today I may try to make everything I do fit for him to see, and everything I say fit for him to hear.

All this I ask for your love's sake. Amen.

EVENING

O God, before I go to sleep, I want to thank you for
everything I have:

> For this bed in which I lie and this room with its
> comfort;
>
> For my home, for the food I eat, and the clothes I
> wear;
>
> For my books and my games and my hobbies and all
> my possessions;
>
> For my teachers and my father and my mother and
> my brothers and my sisters and my friends.

O God, I know that there is hardly one of these things
which I could get for myself. They are all given to me.

Help me to be grateful for them, and to try to deserve
them a little better.

This I ask for Jesus' sake. Amen.

Third Month: Second Week

O God, you have given me life, and I know that you
want me to make something worthwhile out of it.
Help me
    To keep my body fit;
    To keep my mind keen;
    To keep my thoughts pure;
    To keep my words clean and true.
This I ask for Jesus' sake. Amen.

EVENING

Forgive me, O God, for all the wrong things which I have
    done today.
Forgive me for
    Careless work;
    Inattentive study;
    Wasted time;
    Duties shirked.
O God, I really am sorry about all these things. Help
    me to show that I am sorry by doing better tomorrow,
    for Jesus' sake. Amen.

MORNING

O God, take control of me all through today.
Control my tongue,
   so that I may speak
     No angry word;
     No cruel word;
     No untrue word;
     No ugly word.
Control my thoughts,
   so that I may think
     No impure thoughts;
     No bitter, envious, or jealous thoughts;
     No selfish thoughts.
Control my actions,
   so that all through today
     My work may be my best;
     I may never be too busy to lend a hand to those who
       need it;
     I may do nothing of which afterwards I would be
       ashamed.
All this I ask for Jesus' sake. Amen.

EVENING

O God, before I sleep, I ask you to bless the people I love.
Bless and protect
>My father and my mother;
>My brothers and my sisters;
>My friends and my teachers.

Bless and help
>Those who are sad and lonely;
>Those who are ill and who cannot sleep for pain;
>Those who are poor and forgotten and friendless;
>Those who are far away from home;
>Those who are in danger anywhere by land or sea or in the air.

I know you love everyone and I ask you to bless everyone and to bless me, for Jesus' sake. Amen.

Third Month: Fourth Week

MORNING

O God, all through today,
  make me brave enough
    To show that I belong to you;
    To refuse any dishonest or dishonourable thing;
    To refuse to listen to any ugly or impure word;
    To do the right thing, even if others laugh at me.
Help me all through today really and truly to try to live
  remembering Jesus all the time, and not caring what
  anyone says so long as I am true to him.
This I ask for his sake. Amen.

EVENING

O God, forgive me for all wrong things in today.
Forgive me for
    Disobedience to my parents;
    Failure to listen to my teachers;
    Disloyalty to my friends.
Forgive me for
    Being careless and inattentive in school;
    Being disobliging and selfish at home.
Forgive me for being
    A bad advertisement for my school and for my
      church;
    A bad example to others;
    A disappointment to you and to those who love me.
Help me to sleep well tonight and tomorrow give me
  strength to do better.
This I ask for Jesus' sake. Amen.

MORNING

Help me, O God, never to be envious, jealous, grumbling or discontented.

Help me never to take offence, if someone gets the prize which I thought I should have won, the place in the team which I thought should have been given to me, the honour which I thought I should have received.

Help me never to grudge anyone his success, and never to find pleasure in the sight of someone else's failure.

Help me to stop thinking of myself and of my own feelings as the most important things in the world, and help me always to think of others as much, and more than I think of myself.

Hear this my prayer for your love's sake. Amen.

EVENING

O God, help me to keep in purity my actions, my words, and my thoughts.

Help me to do nothing in secret which I would be ashamed to do openly, and keep me from doing things which I would have to hide and to conceal.

So do you control me that I may have every instinct and passion under complete control. Help me always to refuse to listen to anything which would soil my mind, and to reject every invitation to leave the way of honour.

Help me to speak nothing but the truth. Keep my words clean and let no foul or unclean or dirty word ever be in my mouth.

You have promised that the pure in heart will see you; grant me this purity, this privilege and this reward.

This I ask for Jesus' sake. Amen.

MORNING

Give me today, O God, the mind which can really learn.
Give me

> The attentive mind, that I may concentrate all
> the time on what I am hearing or doing;
>
> The retentive mind, that I may not hear and for-
> get, but that I may grasp a thing and remember
> it;
>
> The open mind, that no prejudice may blind me
> to truth I do not wish to see;
>
> The eager mind, that I may not be content to re-
> main as I am, but that every day I may try to add
> something new to my store of knowledge and of
> skill, and something finer to my store of goodness.

This I ask for Jesus' sake. Amen.

EVENING

Forgive me, O God, for all the wrong things that have
been in my life today.

Forgive me

> For being careless and inattentive in learning;
>
> For being thoughtlessly or deliberately cruel and
> unkind to others;
>
> For hurting the people who love me most of all.
>
> For being disobedient to those whom I ought to
> obey, and for being disrespectful to those whom
> I ought to respect;
>
> For disobeying my conscience, and for doing the
> wrong thing when I knew the right thing.

Help me to show that I am really sorry by doing better
tomorrow and by not making the same mistakes again.

This I ask for Jesus' sake. Amen.

MORNING

O God, give me all the simple, basic things which will make me able to be a useful person in this world.

Help me to be

Honest, so that people will be able absolutely to depend on my word;

Conscientious, so that nothing that I do may ever be less than my best;

Punctual, so that I may not waste the time of others by keeping them waiting for me.

Reliable, so that I may never let people down when I promise to do something;

With a sense of responsibility, so that I may always think of how my action will affect not only myself but others also.

Help me to live in the constant memory that you see and hear all that I do and say.

Hear this my prayer for your love's sake. Amen.

EVENING

O God, before I sleep I would remember others.
I ask you to bless
> The sick who will not sleep tonight;
> The sad who are very lonely tonight;
> Those in peril in the storms at sea;
> Those who are travelling by land or in the air;
> Those in prison and in disgrace;
> Those who have no house and no home of their own;
> Those on national service in the navy, the army, and the air force.

Bless all my friends and loved ones whose names I lay before you now . . . .
Hear this my prayer through Jesus Christ my Lord. Amen.

Fourth Month: Fourth Week

MORNING

Help me, O God, to bear well the things which are hard to bear.

Help me to bear

Pain with cheerfulness and without complaint;

Failure with the perseverance to go on trying until I succeed;

Disappointment without bitterness and without resentment;

Delays with the patience which has learned to wait;

Criticism without losing my temper;

Defeat without making excuses.

Help me to bear the yoke in my youth, that I may make something worthwhile out of life when I grow up.

This I ask for Jesus' sake. Amen.

Fourth Month: Fourth Week

EVENING

Thank you, O God, for all the gifts which have made
today and every day so wonderful.

Thank you for books to read, wise books to make me
wise, books full of information to make me informed;
great stories to thrill the heart and to linger in the
memory; poetry with all its beauty.

Thank you for music of every kind, for dramas and for
plays and for films, for pictures and for sculpture and
for every lovely thing.

Thank you for games to play; for clubs and for fellow-
ships where I can meet and talk and argue and play
with others.

Thank you for
My school in which to learn;
My home in which to love and to be loved;
My Church in which to worship.

Glory and thanks and praise be to you for all your
kindness and your goodness to me.

Hear this my prayer for your love's sake. Amen.

MORNING

Help me to be a good son, and to bring joy and pride
to my parents,

> To work hard, so that I will not disappoint those
> who have high hopes for me;
> To show that I am grateful for all that my parents
> have done for me, and sometimes to tell them so;
> To be obedient to them, and always to give them
> the loving respect I ought to give;
> Never to use my home simply for my own con-
> venience, but to be a real partner in it, and to try
> to put into it more than I take out.

Help me always to honour my father and mother as
your law commands.

This I ask for Jesus' sake. Amen.

EVENING

Help me, O God, to be a good and a true friend,

> To be always loyal, and never to let my friends
> down;
> Never to talk about them behind their backs in a
> way in which I would not do before their faces;
> Never to betray a confidence or talk about the things
> about which I ought to be silent;
> Always to be ready to share everything I have;
> To be as true to my friends as I would wish them
> to be to me.

This I ask for the sake of him who is the greatest and the
truest of all friends, for Jesus' sake. Amen.

MORNING

Help me, O God, to be a good scholar and pupil of my
school,

> To study with concentration;
>
> To do my work with diligence and care;
>
> To be obedient and respectful to my teachers;
>
> To take my full part in the life and the activities of
> my school;
>
> To take full advantage of all the opportunities given
> to me to learn; and to make myself a good
> craftsman and a good citizen of my country when
> I leave school and go out to work;

This I ask for the sake of him who was the greatest of all
teachers, for Jesus' sake. Amen.

EVENING

Help me, O God, to be a good sportsman and a good
member of my team,

> To accept discipline and to train strictly;
>
> To play hard but to play fair;
>
> To play the game for the good of the team and not
> for my own honour and glory.
>
> To obey instructions without arguing;
>
> Not to resent it if I am dropped from the team
> because someone else is preferred;
>
> To be a credit to my colours wherever I play and
> wherever I go.

This I ask for Jesus' sake. Amen.

Fifth Month: Third Week

O Lord Jesus, help me to be a good follower of you,
Always to follow your example;
Always to ask what you want me to do before I decide to do anything;
Always to ask for your help and your guidance;
Always to remember that you are always with me to hear what I say, to see what I do, to keep me from doing wrong, and to give me the help I need to do the right:
Never to be afraid to show my loyalty to you, and never to be ashamed to show that I belong to you;
Never to forget all that you have done for me, and so to try to love you as you first loved me.

This I ask for your love's sake. Amen.

EVENING

O God, forgive me for all the things that I have left undone today; and forgive me for the things I have left half-finished and for the things which I never even started.

Forgive me for not saying 'Thank you' to the people who have helped me, and for not saying that I am sorry to the people whom I wronged and hurt.

Forgive me if I have hurt anyone, or disappointed anyone, or if I have caused anyone trouble, or if I have been a bad example to anyone.

Give me your help tomorrow, so that I may leave nothing undone of the things I ought to do, and so that I may do none of the things I ought not to do.

This I ask for your love's sake. Amen.

MORNING

Help me, O God, always to take the long view of things.

Keep me from ever doing on the impulse of the moment
things for which I would be very sorry afterwards.

Help me to remember that, even if at the moment I
would rather play and amuse myself than work or
study, I must accept the discipline of work, if I am to
make anything worthwhile out of life.

Especially keep me from any habits or indulgences or
pleasures which would injure others and hurt myself,
and which some day I would bitterly regret.

Help me to look beyond this moment, and even to look
beyond this world, and so help me to remember that
this life is not the end, and help me always to live in
such a way that, when this life does end, I may hear
you say, ' Well done! '

Hear this my prayer through Jesus Christ my Lord.
Amen.

EVENING

O God, tonight I want to pray to you for people who
have to suffer and to sacrifice for their Christian faith.
I ask you to bless

> Missionaries who go out to other lands to tell the
> story of Jesus to those who have never heard it,
> and who have to endure discomforts, face dangers,
> and accept long months and years of separation
> from those whom they love;

> People who live in countries in which Christians are
> hated and hunted and persecuted for their faith,
> and specially Christians who live in countries in
> which they are persecuted and cruelly treated by
> others who also call themselves Christians but
> who belong to a different Church;

> People who live or work in circumstances in which
> they are laughed at and even despised for trying
> to live a Christian life.

This I ask for your love's sake. Amen.

' The fruit of the Spirit is love, joy, peace, patience, kindness, goodness, faithfulness, gentleness and self-control.' That is what Paul wrote to his friends in the Churches of Galatia (Galatians 5: 22, 23). Let us all through this month ask God to give us these lovely things in our lives.

O God, give me in my life the fruit of love.

Help me to love you so much that I will never forget all that you have given me and all that you have done for me. Help me always to remember that you gave me life and everything that makes life worth living, and that you gave me Jesus to be my Friend, my Example, my Master, and my Saviour. Help me to love my fellow-men so much that I will no longer be selfish and self-centred, but that I will find the way to happiness in doing things for others. This I ask for your love's sake. Amen.

O God, give me in my life the fruit of joy.

Help me always to be happy and cheerful. Help me still to smile even when things go wrong. Help me always to look on the bright side of things, and always to remember that, even when things are at their worst, there is still something to be thankful for. Don't let me grumble and complain; don't let me be a pessimist and a wet blanket.

And help me to find my happiness, not in doing what I want, but in doing what you want, and not in thinking of myself, but in thinking of others, through Jesus Christ my Lord. Amen.

O God, give me in my life the fruit of peace.

Help me to take things calmly. Help me not to get into a panic when things go wrong. Help me not to worry but to take things as they come, a day at a time. Help me not to be nervous but to keep cool, when I have something difficult or important to do.

Help me never to lose my temper, no matter how annoying things or people may be.

Keep me calm and steady, so that I will never collapse, and so that others may be able to rely on me when they are up against it. This I ask for Jesus' sake. Amen.

O God, give me in my life the fruit of patience.

Help me to have patience at my work and study, so that I will never give in but always persevere.

Help me to have patience with people, so that I may never lose my temper and never grow cross or irritable, or blaze into angry words. Help me to have patience when things are slow to come and slow to happen.

Help me to have patience not to give up, when something takes a long time to do, and when it does not come out right the first or the second time.

Help me to remember that everything worth doing is hard to do; that everything worth getting is hard to get; that everything worth being is hard to be, but that the struggle and the effort are worthwhile in the end.

This I ask for Jesus' sake. Amen.

O God, give me in my life the fruit of kindness.

Make me quick to see what I can do for others, and make me eager and willing to do it. Make me always obliging and always willing to lend a hand. Help me never to be mean, but always to be ready to share everything I have, even if I have not got very much.

Help me never to speak unkind words and never to do cruel deeds. Help me to think the best of others, and always to be more willing to forgive than to condemn.

Help me to be as kind to others as I would wish them to be to me.

Hear this my prayer for your love's sake. Amen.

O God, give me in my life the fruit of goodness.

Help me to be in everything I do and say a good example to others, and help me never to do anything which would make it easier for someone else to go wrong.

Keep my words honest and pure. Keep my actions fit for you to see, and help me never to do anything that I would wish to keep secret, and that I would be afraid that other people would find out about. Keep all my thoughts clean, so that even the most secret of them would bear the full light of day.

And in everything keep me from pride and from self-conceit; and help me to think, not of what I know, but of what I don't know; not of what I have done, but of what I have still to do; not of what I am, but of what I ought to be.

Hear this my prayer for Jesus' sake. Amen.

O God, give me in my life the fruit of faithfulness.

> Keep me always true to myself, true to my friends, true to those who love me and true to you.
>
> Grant that nothing may ever make me tell a lie. If I give my promise, grant that nothing may ever make me break it. If I say that I will do something, grant that others may be able to rely absolutely on me to do it. Help me always to stand by my friends and never to let them down, and help me never to grieve or to disappoint those who love me and those whom I love.
>
> Make me so straight, so honourable and so true that everyone will be able to trust me in small things and in great alike. This I ask through Jesus Christ my Lord. Amen.

O God, give me in my life the fruit of gentleness.

> Help me never to speak an angry or a cruel word, and never to do a hurting or a wounding deed.
>
> Grant that I may never find any pleasure in anything which would hurt any person or any animal. Help me to be as careful of the feelings of others as I would wish them to be of mine.
>
> Help me not to be too rough and boisterous in my behaviour with those who are not so strong as I am. And make me specially gentle and thoughtful to those who are sick and sad and old and weak and easily hurt.
>
> This I ask for your love's sake. Amen.

O God, give me in my life the fruit of self-control.

Please take control of me so that I will be able to control myself.

Help me always to control my temper and my tongue. Help me always to control my feelings and my impulses.

Grant that I may never be swept away in some moment of passion into doing something which would hurt anyone else and which all my life I would regret.

Help me to control even my thoughts, so that no bitter thought, no unforgiving thought, no jealous thought, no ugly or unclean thought may ever get into my mind.

Make me master of myself for I know that, unless I can master myself I can never make anything worthwhile out of life.

Hear this my prayer for your love's sake. Amen.

MORNING

Lord Jesus, help me to remember that you are always with me.

Help me to do nothing which would grieve you to see, and nothing which I would be ashamed to think that you should see me doing.

When I am tempted, help me always to ask you for strength to do the right thing and to resist the wrong thing.

When I don't know what to do, help me to turn to you and ask you for your advice.

When I am frightened and lonely, help me to feel that you are there, and to know that with you I don't ever need to be afraid.

Help me to go through life with you as my Friend and my Companion all the time.

This I ask for your love's sake. Amen.

EVENING

O God, forgive me for all the things in me which have
 kept today from being what it might have been.
Forgive me for being
     Inattentive at school;
     Disobliging at home;
     Bad-tempered with my friends;
     Selfish and thoughtless in my conduct.
Help me tomorrow
     To concentrate on learning;
     To honour my father and my mother;
     To be generous and unselfish in everything;
     To be a good comrade to all my friends.
So help me to please you, and not to disappoint those
 who love me.
This I ask for Jesus' sake. Amen.

MORNING

Help me today, O God,
>   To keep my temper and to control my tongue;
>   To keep my thoughts from wandering and my mind
>   from straying;
>   To quarrel with no one and to be friends with
>   everyone.

So bring me to the end of today with nothing to be sorry
for, and with nothing left undone; through Jesus
Christ my Lord. Amen.

EVENING

O God, thank you for taking care of me all through
today.

Thank you for making me able to go out in the morning
in good health, and thank you for giving me my home
and my father and mother to come back to.

Thank you
>   For all that I have learned today;
>   For all the games that I have played today;
>   For all the friends that I have met today.

And thank you for Jesus my Master and my Friend.

Help me to sleep soundly tonight, and to waken fit for
work and play tomorrow; through Jesus Christ my
Lord. Amen.

MORNING

Whatever happens today, help me to keep cheerful.
Help me
> Not to grumble when things go wrong;
> Not to be discouraged when things are difficult;
> Not to get annoyed when I don't get my own way;
> Not to sulk if I get a row for anything wrong that
> I have done.

Help me, hail, rain, or shine, to keep smiling, so that I
may be what you want me to be—a light of the world.
This I ask for your love's sake. Amen.

EVENING

O God, I don't want to pray for myself tonight; I want
to pray for others.
I ask you to bless
> Those who are ill, and whose pain is worse at night;
> Those who are sad, and who are specially lonely
> at night;
> Those who are in strange towns and countries, and
> who are missing their own homes and their own
> people;
> Those in danger at sea, or in the air, or on the land;
> Doctors and nurses, awake and helping others, while
> we sleep;
> All the people I love, and all the people who love me.

And bless me and keep me safe all through the night
until the morning comes again; through Jesus Christ
my Lord. Amen.

MORNING

O God, help me never to allow any habit to get such a grip of me that I cannot break it.

Specially keep me from all habits which would injure my body or my mind.

Help me always to do my best with your help to keep my body fit and healthy, and my mind clean and pure.

Help me at present to discipline and to train myself, to learn and to study, so that some day I may be able to do something worthwhile for the world and for you; through Jesus Christ my Lord. Amen.

EVENING

O God, forgive me for all the wrong things that I have
done today.

Forgive me

For blaming others for things which were entirely
my own fault;

For being rude, and discourteous, and bad-
tempered, especially at home;

For being rough, and unkind, and unjust.

Forgive me

For the things which I should have done and have
not done;

For the times I lost my temper and my patience;

For the lessons I have left unprepared and the tasks
I have left half-done or badly done;

For the things I promised to do and did not do.

The trouble is that I know what I ought to do, and I
really mean to do it, but somehow it does not turn
out that way.

Forgive me, and help me tomorrow

To do what I know I ought to do,

And to be what I know I ought to be.

This I ask for your love's sake. Amen.

MORNING

Even before Christianity came into the world men have always believed that the four greatest virtues are WISDOM, COURAGE, JUSTICE and SELF-CONTROL. Let us ask God to help us to have them in our lives.

O God, help me to have in my life the virtues which all men value and admire.

Give me wisdom always to know

What I ought to do;

What I ought to say;

Where I ought to go.

Give me courage,

To do the right thing when it is difficult;

If need be, to be laughed at for my faith;

Never to be ashamed to show my loyalty to you.

Give me justice,

Always to be fair in thought and word and action;

Always to think of the rights of others as much as of my own;

Never to be content when anyone is being unjustly treated.

Give me self-control,

Always to have my impulses, passions and emotions under perfect control;

Never to be swept into doing things for which I would be sorry;

Never to do anything which would hurt others, grieve those who love me, or bring shame to myself.

Hear this my prayer for your love's sake   Amen.

EVENING

Forgive me, O God,
>   For the time I have wasted today;
>   For the people I have hurt today;
>   For the tasks I have shirked today.
Help me
>   Not to be discouraged when things are difficult;
>   Not to be content with second bests;
>   To do better tomorrow than I have done today.
And help me always to remember that Jesus is with me
>   and that I am not trying all alone.
This I ask for Jesus' sake. Amen.

MORNING

O God, keep me from allowing any habit to get such a grip of me that I can't stop it.

Keep me from becoming so fond of any pleasure that I can't do without it.

Keep me from allowing myself to become lazy, and from getting into a state in which I don't really care whether things are well or badly done.

Keep me from allowing myself to do things which would make it easier for me to go wrong and which would be a bad example to others.

Help me to live in purity and in self-discipline, and in the memory that you are always with me to see what I do, and to help me to overcome wrong and to do the right; through Jesus Christ my Lord. Amen.

EVENING

Forgive me, O God, for all the opportunities that I have missed today: opportunities to learn more; to gain a little more knowledge or skill for my mind; to help people who need help; to say a word of praise or thanks or congratulation; to show those who love me that I love them.

Help me to remember that opportunities so often only come once, and help me from this time on to seize them when they come; through Jesus Christ my Lord. Amen.

MORNING

O God, your word tells me that, whatever my hand finds to do, I must do it with my might.

Help me today to concentrate with my whole attention on whatever I am doing, and keep my thoughts from wandering and my mind from straying.

> When I am studying,
> help me to study with my whole mind.
> When I am playing,
> help me to play with my whole heart.

Help me to do one thing at a time, and to do it well.

This I ask for Jesus' sake. Amen.

EVENING

Thank you, O God, for everything that has happened today:

> For the good things which have made me happy;
> For the not so good things which have taught me that I can't always be getting my own way;
> For successes to give me happy things to remember;
> For failures to keep me humble;
> For time at work, at school, at games,
> with my friends and in my own home.

And thank you for this minute with you. Help me to go to sleep thinking about you that I may rise tomorrow to live obedient and true to you; through Jesus Christ my Lord. Amen.

MORNING

O God, help me to be cheerful all through today,
> Whatever I have to do, help me to do it with a smile.

O God, help me to be diligent all through today,
> Whatever I have to do, help me to do my best.

O God, help me to be kind all through today,
> Whatever I have to do, help me not to be too busy to help someone else.

O God, help me to be brave all through today,
> Whatever I have to do, help me to face it and not to dodge it.

O God, help me to be reverent all through today,
> Whatever I have to do, help me to remember that you see me, and help me to make every word fit for you to hear, and every bit of work fit to offer to you.

This I ask for your love's sake. Amen.

EVENING

O God, bless all the people who are in trouble tonight, those who cannot sleep because they are ill and in pain, or because they are old and lonely, or because they are worried and nervous and anxious.

Bless any who are in danger.

Bless those who must work at night,
> doctors on call, nurses in hospital and infirmary wards, policemen on the beat, those called out to accidents, fires, shipwrecks.

Bless me now, and help me to sleep well tonight and to waken tomorrow to live strong and true; through Jesus Christ my Lord. Amen.

MORNING

O God, my Father, thank you for all the ordinary, every-
day things of life.

Thank you,

> For food and for a good appetite to enjoy it;
> For games and for physical fitness to play them;
> For lessons and for a mind to learn and to think, and
> for a memory to remember;
> For work and for strength and skill to do it.

Help me always

> To keep my body clean and fit;
> To keep my mind keen and alert;
> To give my heart to you, because you have loved
> me so much and have done so much for me.

This I ask for Jesus' sake. Amen.

EVENING

O God, before I go to sleep tonight I am looking back
across today.

Thank you,

> For any new thing I have learned today;
> For any good thing I have been able to do today;
> For any happiness I have brought today to those
> who love me and who want me to do well.

Forgive me

> For anything I have shirked today;
> For anything I have put off today;
> For anything which I have could have done better
> today;
> For anyone whom I have hurt or disappointed
> today.

Help me to sleep well tonight and to do better tomorrow.

This I ask for your love's sake. Amen.

MORNING

O God, my Father, give me all through today sound
sense to see what it is right to do, and strength of will
and purpose to do it. And, if I am not able to do it
the first time, give me perseverance to keep on trying.

O God, my Father, give me all through today an eye
which is quick to see what I can do for others, and
willingness to do it.

Help me not to do things with a grudge; and help me
to do what I am told to do at once, and not to need to
be told to do it again and again.

Help me today to bring happiness wherever I go, so that
I may find my own happiness in making others happy;
through Jesus Christ my Lord. Amen.

EVENING

O God, thank you for all the people who have been kind to me today.

Thank you for the people who have patience with me when I am irritating and annoying, and who don't lose their temper with me when I lose mine with them.

Thank you for the people who have patience with me when I am slow to learn and slow to take things in, and who don't give me up as hopeless, when I seem to make no progress at all.

Thank you for those who give me, not what I deserve, but far more than I deserve.

Thank you for those who keep on loving me even when I hurt and disappoint them.

Help me to try to bring joy to those who do so much for me, by trying to be what they want me to be; through Jesus Christ my Lord. Amen.

MORNING

O God, help me to think all through today in every word and in every action and in every situation of what Jesus would do.

Help me to think of how Jesus went to school and learned and grew in wisdom, just as I must do.

Help me to think how he worked in the carpenter's shop and learned a trade, just as I must do.

Help me to remember how he obeyed his parents, just as I must do.

Help me to remember how he found people unjust and unfair and unsympathetic and unkind, just as may happen to me.

Help me to remember how his friends let him down, just as may happen to me.

Help me to remember that he loved us all so much that he gave for us everything he had, even his life, just as I ought to do.

He has left us an example that we should follow in his steps. Help me to follow in his steps all through today. This I ask for your love's sake. Amen.

EVENING

O God, forgive me for all the things which have defeated
me today.

For the times

    When I knew that I ought to do something, and when
      I was too lazy to do it;

    When I knew that I ought to help someone, and
      when I was too lazy to be bothered;

    When I knew that I ought to keep quiet, and when
      I let my tongue run away with me;

    When I knew that I ought to keep my temper, and
      when I let it flare up and blaze out;

    When I knew I ought to speak, and when I remained
      silent because I was too much of a coward to
      speak.

O God, I always start in the morning meaning to do so
well, and I seem always to finish at night after doing
so badly. Forgive me; help me; and, whatever
happens, don't let me stop trying.

This I ask for Jesus' sake. Amen.

Ninth Month: Fourth Week

FOR SUNDAY MORNING

O God, help me to remember that this is your day, and
help me to use it differently from the other days.

Help me to use it to learn something more about Jesus
and to come to know him a little better.

Help me to use it to go to Church to sing and pray and
listen and worship with those who are the friends of
Jesus.

Help me to use it to do something for others—those who
are ill, those who are old, and those who are lonely.

Help me to use Sunday in such a way as to help me to
live better through all the other days of the week:
through Jesus Christ my Lord. Amen.

BEFORE GOING TO CHURCH

O God, in Church today help me to listen, to understand and to remember.

Help me to go to Church reverently, because the Church is your house and you are specially there.

When we all pray, grant that it may be just like speaking to you.

When I listen, help me to concentrate so that I will really hear and take in and remember what is said.

And then help me to go out and to put into practice all you tell me in your house.

This I ask for your love's sake. Amen.

MORNING

O God, my Father, help me today not to let anyone or
anything stop me from being what I ought to be and
doing what I ought to do.

> Even if people are nasty to me, help me to be
> courteous to them.

> Even if people are unkind to me, help me to be
> loving and kind to them.

> Even if people hurt me or insult me or injure me,
> help me to forgive them as Jesus forgave those
> who were crucifying him.

> Even if things and people make it very difficult for
> me to do what I know I ought to do, help me still
> at least to try to do it.

Lord Jesus, help me to live today in perfect loyalty and
obedience to you.

This I ask for your love's sake. Amen.

EVENING

Forgive me, O God, for everything in which I have failed today.

Forgive me for

Losing my temper when I should have controlled it;

Allowing my tongue to run away with me when I should have kept quiet;

Allowing myself to have bitter feelings about someone else;

Refusing to listen to good advice and for resenting correction when I deserved it.

Forgive me for

Failing to do things as well as I could have done them,

Failing to finish the tasks I should have finished;

Failing to work my hardest at my lessons and my work, and to play my hardest at my games.

Forgive me for everything that I meant to do and failed to do, and for everything that I meant not to do and did.

This I ask for Jesus' sake. Amen.

MORNING

O God, help me to live well today.

Help me

    To do my work diligently;

    To face my temptations victoriously;

    To play my games whole-heartedly;

    To bear my disappointments cheerfully;

    To face my difficulties manfully;

    To give all the help I can to all the people I can willingly;

    To obey you faithfully;

    And to follow Jesus loyally.

All this I ask for Jesus' sake. Amen.

EVENING

O God, thank you for giving me another day of life.
Thank you for
> The things I have learned today;
> The games I have played today;
> The friends I have met today;

Thank you for
> The love and care I have received today in my home;
> The teaching and training I have received today in my school;
> The loyalty and friendship I have received today from my comrades.

Thank you most of all for Jesus,
> The Example whom I must copy;
> The Friend who never leaves me;
> The Saviour who forgives me and makes me able to live well.

Hear this my prayer, and give me always a grateful heart; through Jesus Christ my Lord. Amen.

MORNING

O God, I ask you to bless all the people who today will have to do very difficult things and face very great responsibilities:

> Statesmen who will have to make decisions on which the welfare of nations and even of the world depends;
>
> Doctors and surgeons in whose hands and whose skill are the lives of men and women and boys and girls;
>
> Those whose job makes them responsible for the safety and the lives of others;
>
> Those who are in positions in which by speaking or by writing or by their example they can influence the lives of thousands of people;
>
> Bless all such.

Bless me. You have given me this life and I am responsible to you for how I use it. Help me to use every moment of today's time and every ounce of today's strength wisely and well; through Jesus Christ my Lord. Amen.

EVENING

O God, help me to sleep well tonight.

And bless those for whom there will be no sleep tonight:

Policemen on the beat;

Workers on the night-shift;

Sailors at sea, engine-drivers on the railways, motor-drivers on the roads, pilots in the air;

All who through the night look after the essential public services on which our convenience and comfort depend;

Doctors and surgeons and nurses, easing the pain or fighting for the life of those who are desperately ill;

Mothers with children who cannot sleep.

O God, I know that you never slumber or sleep. Through the dark hours give me sleep and watch over me while I sleep, and be with those who work while others sleep.

This I ask for Jesus' sake. Amen.

MORNING

O God, give me all through today
> Grace willingly to say Yes, when I am asked to help someone else;
>
> Strength resolutely to say No, when I am tempted or persuaded to do anything that is wrong;
>
> Patience to say to myself Wait, when I am in too big a hurry;
>
> Resolution to say Now, when I am inclined to put off till some future time what should be done today;
>
> Obedience to say to you, Lord, What do you want me to do? in every choice which comes to me today.

Hear this my prayer through Jesus Christ my Lord. Amen.

EVENING

O God, thank you for today.
Thank you for

>Lessons and tasks which stretched my mind, and made it able to cope with still more difficult things;

>Training and games which left me tired, but fit for bigger efforts;

>Kindness which touched my heart and made me love people and be grateful to them more than ever;

>Anything in the world or in the things which happened today which made me think of you.

Thank you for the good things which I will never forget, and forgive me for the bad things which I would like to forget; through Jesus Christ my Lord. Amen.

Eleventh Month: First Week

MORNING

O God, my Father, help me to do the things which are
very difficult for anyone to do.

    To be obedient,
      When I would like my own way;
    To persevere,
      When I am tired and discouraged,
      And when I would like to give up;
    To study,
      When I would like to be out playing games;
    To help with the work of the house,
      When I think that it is a nuisance,
      And when I can't be bothered;
    To keep my temper,
      When I would like to blaze out,
      And tell people just what I think of them;
    To forgive,
      When I am feeling hurt and sore and bitter;
        Help me to do these things.

At all times help me to find my happiness in obeying
you.

This I ask for your love's sake. Amen.

EVENING

Forgive me, O God, for all the wrong things I have done today.

Forgive me

For forgetting the things I ought to have remembered;

For failing to do the things I promised to do;

For being inattentive to the things to which I should have listened;

For being careless with the work on which I should have concentrated;

Forgive me, O God.

Forgive me

For doing things which I knew would annoy people;

For behaving in a way that I knew would hurt people;

For doing things that I knew would disappoint people;

Forgive me, O God.

O God, when I look back, I can see now how foolish and how wrong I have been. Forgive me, and help me not to do the same things again. This I ask for Jesus' sake. Amen.

MORNING

Help me, O God, not to waste my time and energy on
useless things.

Help me

Not to envy others their gifts,
But to make the best of the gifts I have;
Never to wish that I was someone else or somewhere
else,
But to do the best I can as I am, and where I am;
Never to be jealous of anyone else,
But to be glad when others do well,
Not to worry about things,
But to take them as they come;
Never to be lost in dreams and schemes and plans,
Without doing anything to make them come true.

Help me to use my strength and my time wisely, bravely
and unselfishly, so that I will make the best of life for
myself and for others; through Jesus Christ my Lord.
Amen

Eleventh Month: Second Week

EVENING

O God, forgive me
    For hurting my parents today;
    For causing trouble to my teachers today;
    For failing to help my friends today.
Forgive me
    For being discourteous in my conduct today;
    For being unkind in my words today;
    For being unjust in my thoughts today.
Forgive me
    For the things I put off;
    For the things I did in too big a hurry to do them
      well;
    For the things I have left half-done;
    For the things I should not have done at all.
Forgive me, and help me to do better tomorrow: for
  Jesus' sake. Amen.

MORNING

O God, my Father, thank you for the world in which
    I live.
Thank you
    For all the beautiful things in it;
    For all the interesting things in it;
    For all the useful things in it.
Thank you for the life which you have given me.
Thank you for
    My body to act;
    My mind to think;
    My memory to remember;
    My heart to love.
Thank you for giving me
    So many things to enjoy;
    So many things to learn;
    So many things to do;
    So many people to love.
Help me never to do anything which would make the
    world uglier or people sadder. Help me always to
    add something to the world's beauty and to the world's
    joy: through Jesus Christ my Lord. Amen.

EVENING

O God, bless all the people who are in trouble tonight.
Bless

> Those who are sad because someone they loved has
> died today;
>
> Those who are anxious because someone they love
> is ill today;
>
> Those who are lonely because someone they love
> left home today.

Bless

> Those who are tired because they have too much to
> do;
>
> Those who are poor and badly paid, and who have
> to do without the things they really need;
>
> Those who are unhappy because someone has been
> unkind and cruel to them.

Help me never to be selfish and never to forget all about
the people who are not so fortunate as I am. Help me
always to remember the needs of others and to do what
I can to help; through Jesus Christ my Lord. Amen.

MORNING

Give me, O God, a sense of responsibility.
Give me
> A sense of responsibility to myself,
>> So that I may never waste the gifts which you have given to me;
>
> A sense of responsibility to my parents,
>> So that I may do something to try to repay them for all the love and the care they have given to me;
>
> A sense of responsibility to my teachers,
>> So that all their patient teaching of me may not go for nothing;
>
> A sense of responsibility to my friends,
>> So that I may never disappoint them;
>
> A sense of responsibility to those who have gone before me,
>> So that I may never forget what my freedom and liberty cost, and so that I may hand on still finer the heritage and the tradition into which I have entered;
>
> A sense of responsibility to the world,
>> So that I may put into life more than I take out;
>
> A sense of responsibility to Jesus,
>> So that I may always remember that he loved me and gave himself for me.

Help me to remember what I have received, and to use what I have, and so to make what I ought out of this life of mine, which cost so much.

This I ask for Jesus' sake. Amen.

EVENING

Forgive me, O God, for all the times when I was a trouble and a nuisance to people today.

Forgive me

For times when I was stubborn and obstinate;

For times when I was careless and forgetful;

For times when I was disobliging and unhelpful;

For times when I was far slower to learn than I need have been;

For times when I was late and kept people waiting;

For times when I argued when I should have kept quiet;

For times when I got in the way, and hindered people and kept them back;

For times when I made things unpleasant when I did not get my own way.

Help me from now on always to make things easier and not more difficult for the people with whom I live and work, and to help people on the way instead of getting in their way.

This I ask for your love's sake. Amen.

MORNING

O God, give me a sense of responsibility.
Keep me
> From doing things without thinking;
> From leaving an untidy mess behind me wherever I go;
> From being carelessly or deliberately destructive;
> From not caring how much worry and anxiety I cause other people;
> From not even beginning to realize all that I get, and all that is done for me, and all that it costs to give it to me;
> From failing to grasp the opportunities which are offered to me;
> From failing to realize the difference between the things which are important and the things which do not matter.

Help me
> Always to use my time and my life wisely and well;
> Always to be considerate of others;
> Always to realize all that is done for me, and to show by my good and cheerful conduct that I am grateful for it.

Hear this my prayer for Jesus' sake. Amen.

EVENING

O God, I know that you like a good workman, and I
don't think that I have been very good today.
I am remembering now
    Things I haven't done at all;
    Things I have left half-done and unfinished;
    Things I didn't do very well, not nearly as well as
        I could have done them;
    Things I did with a grudge;
    Things I put off, and things I refused to do.
Forgive me for all bad workmanship, and help me to do
    better tomorrow; through Jesus Christ my Lord.
    Amen.

MORNING

Help me, O God, not to be impatient when older people
tell me what to do and what not to do, even though
they often tell me to do things I don't want to do,
and to stop doing things I do want to do.

Help me to remember that they know what life is like,
and that they know from experience the things which
are wise and the things which are bound to cause
trouble.

And help me to remember, when I think that they are
hard on me, that it is not because they don't like me
but because they do like me, and because they want
to save me from mistakes and to see me do well.

So help me always to be obedient and always to listen
to advice.

This I ask for Jesus' sake. Amen.

EVENING

Forgive me, O God, for everything that has gone wrong
today.

Forgive me

For being cheeky to my parents;

For being careless with my lessons;

For quarrelling with my friends;

For causing people extra work and extra trouble;

For grumbling and complaining about things which
I knew that I would have to do in the end anyway.

Help me tomorrow to make life more pleasant for myself
and for everyone I live with and everyone I meet;
through Jesus Christ my Lord. Amen.

MORNING

Give me, O God, a will that is strong and steady.
Help me
> Not to give up so easily,
>> but to stick at things until I succeed in doing
>> them;
> Not to be so easily annoyed,
>> but to keep calm, and to take things as they come;
> Not to be so easily led,
>> but to be able to stand alone, and, if necessary,
>> to say No, and to keep on saying No;
> Not to lose interest so quickly,
>> but to concentrate on everything I do,
>> and to finish everything I begin.

Give me a will strong enough always to choose the right,
and never to be persuaded to anything that is wrong;
through Jesus Christ my Lord. Amen.

EVENING

Bless those who are ill, and who cannot sleep tonight
because of their pain.

Bless those who are in hospitals, in infirmaries, and in
nursing-homes; and bless the doctors and the nurses
who are trying to help and to cure them.

Bless those who are sad and lonely.

Bless those who are in prison and all those who are in
any kind of trouble or disgrace.

Bless those who are far away from home, amongst strange
people in a strange place.

Bless all those whom I love and all those who love me.

Bless me and help me to sleep well tonight.

This I ask for Jesus' sake. Amen.

MORNING

O God, bless my school, the headmaster, the teachers, the scholars and everybody in it.

Help us all to work so hard and to play so well that everyone will respect and admire our school.

When I am in school, help me to be a good and attentive scholar, and, when I am out of school, help me always to behave in such a way that I will always be a credit to the badge and to the colours which I wear.

Help me to remember all the time that I am at school that I am preparing myself to be a good citizen of this country, and a good servant of yours; and to that end help me

> To discipline my mind to be wise;
> To train my body to be fit;
> To equip my life to be useful.

Hear this my prayer for your love's sake. Amen.

EVENING

O God, thank you for keeping me safe all day today from the time I got up in the morning until now it is time to go to bed and to sleep.

Thank you,

> For giving me health and strength to work and to play;
>
> For giving me food to eat, clothes to wear, and a home to live in;
>
> For giving me parents to care for me, teachers to instruct me, friends to work and to play with me;
>
> For bringing me to this night, and for giving me sleep and a bed to sleep in;
>
> For giving me Jesus to be my Master and my Friend, and to be with me all through the day and all through the night.

And grant that the memory of his presence may keep me from all wrong things by day and from all fear by night.

This I ask for your love's sake. Amen.

Essential
Prague

by Christopher and Melanie Rice

Since Christopher completed his PhD in
Russian history, he and Melanie have
travelled widely and have written numerous
travel guides. Their titles for AA Publishing
include *Essential Austria*, *Essential Budapest*,
CityPack Moscow, *CityPack Istanbul*,
AA/Thomas Cook Travellers Berlin,
Explorer Moscow and St Petersburg and,
most recently, *Explorer Turkish Coast*. The
Rices first visited Prague at the time of the
Velvet Revolution and have watched
developments since with fascination. They
now live in London with their two children.

Above: *Národní divaldo (National Theatre)* foyer ceiling
painting

AA Publishing

Above: a *hat seller*

Written by Christopher and Melanie Rice

Published and distributed in the United Kingdom by AA
Publishing, a trading name of Automobile Association
Developments Limited, whose registered office is Norfolk
House, Priestley Road, Basingstoke, Hampshire, RG24
9NY.
Registered number 1878835.

© Automobile Association Developments Limited
1998, 2001
Maps © Automobile Association Developments
Limited 1998
**Reprinted 2001. Information verified and
updated.**

Automobile Association Developments Limited
retains the copyright in the original edition © 1998
and in all subsequent editions, reprints and
amendments.

A CIP catalogue record for this book is available from the
British Library.

ISBN 0 7495 3128 2

The contents of this publication are believed correct at
the time of printing. Nevertheless, the publishers cannot
be held responsible for any errors or omissions or for
changes in the details given in this guide or for the
consequences of any reliance on the information it
provides. Assessments of attractions, hotels, restaurants
and other sights are based upon the author's personal
experience and, therefore, necessarily contain elements of
subjective opinion which may not reflect the publisher's
opinion or dictate a reader's own experience on another
occasion.

We have tried to ensure accuracy in this guide, but
things do change and we would be grateful if readers
would advise us of any inaccuracies they may encounter.

Find out more about
AA Publishing and the
wide range of services
the AA provides by
visiting our website at
www.theAA.com

Colour separation: BTB Digital Imaging Ltd,
Whitchurch, Hampshire
Printed and bound in Italy by Printer Trento S.r.l.

Contents

About this Book

Essential *Prague* is divided into five sections to cover the most important aspects of your visit to Prague.

Viewing Prague pages 5–14
An introduction to Prague by the author
  Prague's Features
  Essence of Prague
  The Shaping of Prague
  Peace and Quiet
  Prague's Famous

Top Ten pages 15–26
The author's choice of the Top Ten places to see in Prague, each with practical information

What to See pages 27–90
Two sections: Prague and Excursions, each with its own brief introduction and an alphabetical listing of the main attractions
  Practical information
  Snippets of 'Did You Know…' information
  4 suggested walks
  2 suggested tours
  2 features

Where To… pages 91–116
Detailed listings of the best places to eat, stay, shop, take the children and be entertained.

Practical Matters pages 117–24
A highly visual section containing essential travel information.

Maps
All map references are to the individual maps found in the What to See section of this guide.
For example, Katedrála Svatého Víta has the reference ➕ 41D2 – indicating the page on which the map is located and the grid square in which the cathedral is to be found. A list of the maps that have been used in this travel guide can be found in the index.

Prices
Where appropriate, an indication of the cost of an establishment is given by **£** signs:
£££ denotes higher prices, **££** denotes average prices, while **£** denotes lower charges.

Star Ratings
Most of the places described in this book have been given a separate rating:
✪✪✪ Do not miss
✪✪ Highly recommended
✪ Worth seeing

Viewing
Prague

Above: *St John of
Nepomuk, Charles
Bridge*
Right: *studying a
map of Praha*

Christopher &t
Melanie Rice's Prague

The Stuff of Novels
In February 1997 the greatest Czech writer of his generation, and one of Prague's most endearing characters, Bohumil Hrabal, fell to his death from a hospital window after climbing out to feed the pigeons. He was 83. For many years Hrabal's second home was the pub U Zlatého Tygra, where he claimed to meet the 'real people' who inspired his novels. His best known work, *Closely Observed Trains*, was made into an Oscar-winning film in 1967.

Praguers know their minds and have always been willing – though not always able – to express them. Standing in Old Town Square, one is reminded of the great Czech religious reformer, Jan Hus, who took on the might of the Catholic Church in order to stand up for what he believed. As so often in the nation's history it was an unequal, albeit heroic, struggle. Over 500 years later, in January 1969, a university student, Jan Palach, suffered a horrific death by self-immolation rather than acquiesce in the Soviet invasion.

Politicians, of course, prefer to leave permanent monuments in brick and stone – the Klementinum, the Charles Bridge, the Valdštejn Palace, Obecní Dům. Everywhere you walk in Prague, its buildings are reminders of the city's history; but they are also aesthetic statements by the architects, artists and sculptors who contributed so much to this most beautiful city. Prague is much more than a glorified museum, however; it is a dynamic place, where individuals are allowed, even encouraged, to stand out from the crowd. To take the city's pulse, spend time in the pubs and cafés that poke out of every nook and cranny. For the traditional view, head for U Zlatého Tygra (► 115), a spit and sawdust, no-nonsense establishment where the customers set the world to rights. But just as representative of today's Prague is Radost FX (► 97), a meeting place for young people from all corners of the world. The growing café culture is symptomatic of the direction the city is taking. Increasingly cosmopolitan and receptive to new ideas, Prague is now more irresistible than ever.

Gregarious Czechs take time out for a game of cards in Václavské náměstí (Wenceslas Square)

Prague's Features

Geography

• Prague lies on the River Vltava at 50° 5' north and 14° 25' east – the heart of Central Europe. The lowest point is 176m above sea level, the highest 396m. Prague is 292km from Vienna, 350km from Berlin, 1,037km from Paris and 1,377km from London.

Climate

• Prague has a mild climate with an average yearly temperature of 9°C. Summers are moderately warm, the hottest months being July and August, when the average temperature reaches 19°C. These are also the wettest months. In January and February, the two coldest months, temperatures hover around 0°C, and there are often sharp frosts.

Population

• Prague covers an area of 497sq km, about two-thirds that of New York, but its population is only 1,210,000, compared with New York City's 8 million. Fewer than 30,000 people (2.5 per cent) live in the historic core of the city; the overwhelming majority inhabit apartment blocks known as *paneláks*, on the outskirts. Approximately 95.5 per cent of the population is of Czech nationality.

Religion

• Although there are hundreds of Roman Catholic and Protestant churches in Prague – 'the city of a thousand spires' (actually 500) – the Czechs are not a deeply religious people. In a recent survey less than 20 per cent admitted to a belief in God.

Tourism

• A new air terminal was opened at Praha Ruzyně, in 1997, to cater for the increasing number of foreign tourists, currently running at approximately 10 million a year. In 1995 foreign exchange receipts from tourism increased by 27 per cent over the previous year, to total 1.7 billion pounds or about 5 per cent of the GDP.

Environment Facts and Figures

Prague has:
10,000 hectares of green space
31km of rivers, 10 islands and 18 bridges
500,000 road vehicles
2,570km of road
130km of tram lines
43km of metro line with 43 stations

Josef Schulz's magnificent Ceremonial Hall is the outstanding architectural feature of the Národní muzeum (National Museum)

Essence of Prague

Two of Prague's many beguiling faces

It is easy to get to know Prague, even to feel at home here. To enjoy the city to the full, be prepared to abandon your sightseeing itinerary whenever the mood takes you – the galleries and museums can wait. Put away the map and wander off the beaten track. Don't neglect the side streets and courtyards, where Prague is often at its most beguiling. To see more, take the tram rather than the metro, and be prepared to go the extra mile: climb to the top of that hill – no city in Europe has more rewarding views.

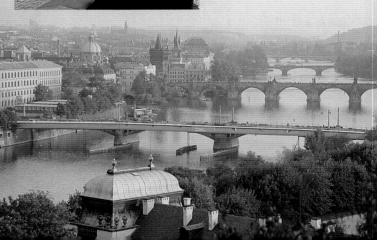

THE **10** ESSENTIALS

*If you only have a short time to visit Prague,
or would like to get a really complete picture of
the city, here are the essentials:*

• **Watch Christ and his Twelve Apostles** signal the hour as they emerge from the Astronomical Clock in Old Town Square (➤ 22).
• **Go to see Kafka's house** in Golden Lane (➤ 73), in the grounds of Prague Castle (➤ 20–1).
• **Listen to the buskers** on the Charles Bridge (➤ 40), while browsing the stalls for souvenirs.
• **Take tram 22** on its scenic journey through the Malá Strana and up to Hradčany.

Veletrzny Palace (➤ 26).
• **Listen to some Mozart** –

• **Take a walk up Wenceslas Square** (➤ 25) stopping to look at Jan Myslbek's famous equestrian statue of St Wenceslas and the small shrine to the martyrs of the Communist era.
• **Visit U Zlatého Tygra** at Jilská 4: a traditional Czech pub, where guests sit at plain wooden tables and wait to be served glasses of the frothy Pilsner Urquell lager (➤ 115).
• **See the Picassos** in the

the real thing at the Estates Theatre (➤ 70) or starring puppets at the National Marionette Theatre (➤ 112).
• **Visit the wonderful Art Nouveau confection, Obecní Dům (➤ 61).** Built as a civic centre in the early 1900s, it has recently been completely renovated.
• **Enjoy the peaceful surroundings** of the Royal Gardens (➤ 50).

Above: *this picturesque cottage in Zlatá ulička (Golden Lane) was once the home of the writer Franz Kafka*
Top: *café life in Staroměstské náměstí (Old Town Square)*

9

The Shaping of Prague

Emperor Rudolph II converses with the astronomer Johannes Kepler

Late 9th century
Prince Bořivoj I builds a timber fort on Hradčany.

*c*935
Duke Wenceslas (later patron saint of Bohemia) is murdered by his brother, Boleslav.

1085
Vratislav II is crowned first King of Bohemia by the Holy Roman Emperor, Henry IV.

1234
Founding of the Staré Město (Old Town), which is fortified with towers, walls and a moat.

1257
Otokar II invites German merchants and tradesmen to settle in the Malá Strana (Lesser Quarter).

1346–78
The reign of Charles IV, Prague's Golden Age. Work begins on St Vitus's Cathedral and the Charles Bridge. The Karolinum (Prague University) and the Nové Město (New Town) are founded.

1415
The religious reformer, Jan Hus, is burnt at the stake for heresy at the Council of Constance in Switzerland.

1419
Hussite rebels throw several city councillors from the windows of the New Town Hall, an incident known to history as the First Defenestration of Prague.

1576–1611
Reign of Emperor Rudolph II. A man of wide and varied interests, he invites the astronomers Tycho Brahe and Johannes Kepler to the city.

1618
Second Defenestration of Prague. Several of Ferdinand II's councillors are hurled from the windows of Prague Castle, this time by Protestant noblemen. The incident triggers the Thirty Years' War.

1620
Battle of the White Mountain. Bohemia's Protestants are defeated and the Counter-Reformation triumphs.

1848
Czech nationalism is strengthened following a revolt by students and workers, which is ruthlessly suppressed by the Austrian General Windischgrätz.

1883
The National Theatre is completed and becomes the cultural focus of opposition to Hapsburg rule.

1914–18
World War I. The Czechs are dragged into the conflict on the Austrian side, although many Czech conscripts desert.

1918
With the defeat of Austria-Hungary, the new Republic of Czechoslovakia is proclaimed in Obecní Dům. Tomáš Masaryk is elected as first president.

1939
Hitler dismembers what remains of Czechoslovakia after the Munich agreement. The Nazis set up the Protectorate of Bohemia and Moravia. Prague's Jews are rounded up and sent to concentration camps.

1939–45
World War II. The German Occupation continues until 1945, when the people of Prague liberate their city and welcome the arrival of the Red Army.

1948
The Communist Party seizes power in what amounts to a *coup d'état*. Beginning of one-party rule and Stalinist repression.

1968
Prime Minister Alexander Dubček introduces the reforms known as 'The Prague Spring'. In August Soviet troops lead the Warsaw Pact invasion of Czechoslovakia.

1977
The dissident playwright, Václav Havel, is one of the founders of Charter '77, a movement protest-ing against the violation of human rights.

1989
'The Velvet Revolution'. After weeks of demonstrations, the Communist government resigns on 10 December and on the 29th Václav Havel is elected president.

1990
Havel's Civic Forum captures more than half the seats in the first free elections.

1993
On 1 January Czechoslovakia splits into separate Czech and Slovak states. Prague becomes the capital of the Czech Republic and Havel begins a new five-year term as president.

1999
The Czechs are formally admitted to NATO and are preparing to enter the European Union.

Sombre memorial to the villagers of Lidice, killed by the Nazis in 1942

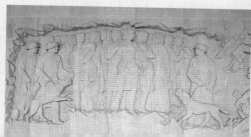

Peace & Quiet

In the City

Prague is fortunate in the variety and proximity of its green spaces, from the wooded hillsides of Petřín and Letná to the public gardens near Wenceslas Square. For a quiet stroll, try the banks of the Vltava at Na Kampě or the former royal hunting grounds of Stromovka (trams 5, 12, 17, 51, 53 or 54 to Holesovice). Keep to the western end (away from the exhibition centre), which was planted as early as 1593, when the lakes and ponds were laid out. The landscaped slopes leading to the Summer Palace of the Czech Governors (1805–11) are a popular spot for picnics.

Krkonoše National Park

Forested paths and peak trails are the main attraction of the Krkonoše (Giant) Mountains, 150km northwest of Prague. One of the most popular routes is along the ridge from Harrachov to Sněžka, following the Polish border. (There are year-round chair lifts to the upper slopes.) This is a good area for bird-watching: alpine accentors and water pipits can be seen on the higher ridges, nutcrackers and woodpeckers on the wooded slopes. The park's administrative centre is at Vrchlabi, but Špindlerův, Mlyn and Rec pod Snežkou are all good bases from which to explore the area.

Slapy Dam

The 65m-high dam across the Vltava River took four years to build and was completed in 1954. The reservoir is a favourite with Prague residents, who flock to the holiday bungalows dotted along its wooded shores to enjoy a weekend's fishing, swimming, boating and water sports. Slapy can be reached directly on route 102, south of Prague, or at a more leisurely pace, by boat (the trip up the Vltava takes four hours).

Stromovka Park is one of Prague's most popular green spaces

Šumava Hills

Forested with beech, fir and spruce, this beautiful area of gently rolling upland lies along the German border. Above the tree line are meadows and grasslands which flower in spring and summer. South of Sušice, a 7km nature trail leads through the scenic Vydra Valley, which can also be reached by road (route 169). Alternatively, take the 163, which follows the course of the Vltava and the impressive

Lipno dam. From here it's a short drive (42km) north again to one of the most beautiful towns of the Czech Republic, Český Krumlov.

The Šumava Hills are an area of great scenic beauty not far from the Czech–German border

The Bohemian Karst

The Karst is a protected area, rich in rare flora – orchids flourish in the slightly acidic limestone soils. Gorges, sinkholes, caves and other unusual rock formations evolved over time due to rainwater erosion, and make for an interesting landscape. Between the castles of Karlštejn and Křivoklát is the stunning Berounka river valley, where red markers indicate rewarding forest trails.

The Bohemian Lakeland

There are more than 6,000 fish ponds in the area around Třeboň, many of them laid out in the 16th century by Štěpánek Netolicky and Mikulas Rathard, fishmasters to the Rožmberks, who owned the land. South of Třeboň is the Svět lake, where locals like to swim and go windsurfing in hot weather. The best way to enjoy the surrounding countryside is to hire a bike – the flat, marshy terrain is a rich habitat for toads and dragonflies and for water birds such as grebes, wildfowl and herons.

Cycling is one of the most enjoyable ways of getting to know the Czech countryside

Prague's Famous

The face of the Czech Republic – President Václav Havel

The Havel Connection
Václav Havel's maternal grandfather, Hugo Vavřecky, was a prominent Prague journalist and diplomat who went on to become managing director of the Bata shoe firm. His highly prized porcelain collection is exhibited at Troja Chateau. Havel's uncle, Miloš, together with Max Urban, founded the Czech film studios at Barrandov in 1933. His paternal grandfather, also called Václav, was a leading avant-garde architect who designed the Lucerna Arcade on Wenceslas Square (► 107).

Václav Havel

Playwright, essayist, former dissident and latterly President of the Czech Republic, Václav Havel also finds time to hobnob with rock celebrities like Mick Jagger, Bob Dylan and Lou Reed. He has been in poor health since undergoing an operation for lung cancer in 1996. Re-elected president two years later, his term of office runs out in January 2003.

Born in Prague on 5 October 1936, Havel turned to the theatre in the late 1950s after being refused a place at the National Film School on ideological grounds. He worked as a lighting technician at the Divadlo Na Zábradlí (Theatre on the Balustrade) and began writing plays. His works were banned after the Soviet invasion and, as a leading dissident, he was a founder member of the human rights movement, Charter 77.

Imprisoned several times, he returned to prominence during the Velvet Revolution and was elected president in December 1989. Shortly after leaving hospital, in January 1997, the president announced that he was marrying the well-known Czech actress, Dagmar Veskrnova, less than a year after the death of his first wife, Olga.

Franz Kafka

One of the 20th century's most influential writers, Franz Kafka was virtually unknown when he died of tuberculosis in 1924 aged 41. Born at U Radnice 5 in 1883, he lived at some 15 addresses in the city, mostly around Old Town Square, where his father owned a haberdasher's shop (Staroměstské náměstí 8). Kafka went to school at the German Gymnasium in the Kinsky Palace before receiving a doctorate in law from the Karolinum in 1906. His student years he wrote in his spare time. His gathering obsession with bureaucratic oppression probably derives from his work as an insurance clerk. In the words of a friend, Johnnes Urzidil, Prague is 'everywhere in Kafka's work, in tiny splinters' – most famously in his short story, *Description of a Struggle*, and the nightmarish novel, *The Castle*, for which the prototype is clearly Pražský hrad.

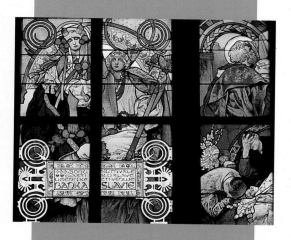

Top Ten

Above: *Katedrála Svatého Víta stained-glass window*
Right: *gate bronzes*

1
Chrám Svatého Mikuláše (St Nicholas's Church)

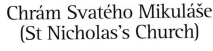

The all-powerful Jesuit Order commissioned this superb church, the ultimate expression of Prague baroque, at the beginning of the 18th century.

🔲 30B2

✉ , Malostranské náměstí

☎ None

🕐 Apr–Oct daily 9–5,
Nov–Mar daily 9–4

🍴 Cafés (£), restaurants
(££–£££) near by

Ⓜ Malostranská

🚌 12, 22

🚇 None

♿ Few

👐 Cheap

↔ Karlův most (➤ 40),
Malostranské náměstí
(➤ 53), Nerudova
(➤ 60), Valdštejnský
palác (➤ 71)

Currently being restored at a cost of 120 million Czech crowns, this monumental building was constructed in 1704–56 by the father-and-son team, Christoph and Kilián Dientzenhofer, and completed by Kilián's son-in-law, Anselmo Lurago. The interior decoration builds on an accumulation of *trompe l'oeil* effects, culminating in *The Apotheosis of St Nicholas* by Johann Kracker, a fresco covering more than 1,500sq m of the nave ceiling. The splendid dome, by Kilián Dietzenhofer, is 18m higher than the Petřín Tower. But not everything is as costly as it appears. Many of the mottled pink and green pillars, cornices and other details, for example, are *faux marbre*, while the four more than life-size statues under the dome are made of wood, with a surface covering of glazed chalk. These dramatic characterisations of the Church Fathers include a vigorous St Cyril triumphantly lancing the devil with his crozier. The sculptor, Ignaz Platzer, also created the copper statue of St Nicholas, which looks down from the high altar. Two other features are worthy of note: the rococo pulpit, overhanging with angels and cherubs, was

Chrám Svatého Mikuláše in the Malá Strana is Prague's most extravagant baroque monument

made by Peter and Richard Práchner in 1765. The baroque organ, played by Mozart in 1787, boasts 2,500 pipes and 44 registers. Four years later it was played at a funeral mass in his memory. The church was full to overflowing, evidence of the esteem in which he was held here.

2
Josefov

For more than 700 years this attractive neighbourhood of the Old Town has been home to Prague's Jewish community.

The Hebrew clock on the roof of the Town Hall in Josefov. There has been a Jewish community in Prague for more than 800 years

Jews first settled in the Old Town in the 12th century. In 1254 the area was surrounded by a ghetto wall, following a decree of the third Lateran Council. The ghetto was a centre of learning, with its own Talmudic school and Hebrew printing press. Although Prague's Jews were regularly subjected to discrimination and persecution, wealthy elders, like Mayor Mordechai Maisel in the 16th century, won privileges for the ghetto by placing their wealth at the disposal of the imperial treasury. In 1784 Emperor Joseph II relaxed many restrictions, and in 1849 Josefov (as the Jewish quarter was now called) was incorporated into the city. Most of the ghetto slums were demolished at the end of the 19th century. The Holocaust all but wiped out the Jewish population of Prague – today's community numbers only about 1,000.

Hitler planned a museum in Josefov recording the history of the 'extinct' Jewish race. Ironically, this ensured the preservation of treasures and furnishings confiscated from synagogues all over Bohemia and Moravia. They are now exhibited in three of the restored synagogues. Other features include a medieval cemetery, and the Old-New Synagogue, which has been the focus of religious worship since the 13th century. Two other museums, the Pinkas Synagogue and the Ceremonial Hall, are impressive memorials to the Holocaust. The former Town Hall, dating from 1763, is a baroque building with a distinctive green steeple. Set in one of the gables is a clock with hands that travel anti-clockwise, following the Hebrew lettering, which is read from right to left.

✝ 31C3

✉ Jáchymova 3, Josefov, Praha 1

☎ 2481 0099 (Jewish Museum)

🕓 Sun–Fri 9–4:30. Closed Jewish hols

🍴 Café (£), restaurant (££) near by

🚇 Staroměstská

🚌 17, 18, 135, 207

🚋 None

♿ Few

✋ Moderate

➡ Anežský klášter (➤ 30–1), Klausová synagóga (➤ 44), Maiselova synagóga (➤ 53), Obřadní síň (➤ 64), Pinkasova synagóga (➤ 65), Staronová synagóga (➤ 69), Starý židovský hřbitov (➤ 69)

17

3
Katedrála Svatého Víta
(St Vitus's Cathedral)

41D2

Pražský hrad, Hradčany, Praha 1

None

Daily 9–5, tower 9–4

Café (£), restaurants (££–£££) near by

None

22

None

Few

Moderate

Pražský hrad (➤ 20–1), Klášter Svatého Jiří (➤ 43)

Additional charge for crypt, tower and choir

St Vitus's took nearly six centuries to complete and was consecrated only in 1929. Yet it stands on the site of a chapel founded in 925.

Work started on the present Gothic building in 1344, under the direction of Matthias of Arras. The German, Petr Parléř (Peter Parler), and his two sons were responsible for the lofty choir and the surrounding chapels, which were finally completed early in the 15th century. The tower on the south side was given its Renaissance steeple in 1562, to which baroque embellishments were later added. The nave and the impressive west end date from the second half of the 19th century. The Golden Portal (the original entrance), on the south side, contains a mosaic of the Last Judgement, dating from 1370, which has recently been restored to its former glory.

The Chapel of St Wenceslas, dating from 1358–67, is one of the oldest parts of the building and the most beautifully decorated. The lower walls are encrusted with scintillating jasper and amethyst, while the frescos (14th–16th centuries) depict scenes from the passion of Christ and the life of St Wenceslas (the saint is buried directly underneath the chapel). The foundations of the 11th-century Romanesque basilica were unearthed as the cathedral was nearing completion and can be seen in the

The soaring Gothic apse of Katedrála Svatého Víta, completed in 1372 by the architect Petr Parléř

crypt, along with the sarcophagi of the kings of Bohemia. King Vladislav Jagiello commissioned the beautiful Royal Oratory in the 1480s: the vaulted ceiling, shaped like the branches of a tree, is highly unusual. An exquisite silver funerary monument to the cult saint, John of Nepomuk, by Fischer von Erlach, was erected in the choir in 1736. One of the cherubs points to the saint's tongue, which was said never to have decayed. The cathedral also contains fine 20th-century stained glass, notably Alfons Mucha's portrait of saints Cyril and Methodius in the third chapel from the west end.

4
Loreta

This pretty baroque shrine has been a place of pilgrimage since 1626, when it was endowed by a Bohemian noblewoman, Kateřina of Lobkowicz.

The Loreta shrine was inspired by a medieval legend. In 1278, so the story goes, the Virgin Mary's house in Nazareth was miraculously transported by angels to Loreto in Italy and thus saved from the Infidel. The Marian cult became an important propaganda weapon of the Counter-Reformation and, following the defeat of the Protestants at the Battle of the White Mountain in 1620, some 50 other Loreto shrines were founded in Bohemia and Moravia.

The heart of the Loreta is the Santa Casa, a replica of the Virgin's relocated house. Sumptuously decorated, it incorporates a beam and several bricks from the Italian original. On the silver altar (behind a grille) is a small ebony statue of the Virgin. The rich stucco reliefs, depicting scenes from the lives of the prophets, are by Italian artists.

The 17th-century cloister of the Loreta, which originally sheltered pilgrims visiting the shrine

The much larger Church of the Nativity was designed by Kilian Dientzenhofer in 1734–5, with ceiling frescos by Václav Reiner and Johann Schöpf. Less edifying are the gruesome remains of saints Felecissimus and Marcia, complete with wax death masks. The cloisters, originally 17th century but with an upper storey added by Dientzenhofer in the 1740s, once provided overnight shelter for pilgrims. In the corner chapel of Our Lady of Sorrows is a diverting painting of St Starosta, a bearded lady who prayed for facial hair to put off an unwanted suitor, only to be crucified by her thwarted father. The Loreta treasury has a famed collection of vestments and other religious objects, including a diamond monstrance made in Vienna in 1699, which glitters with 6,200 precious stones.

✝ 30A3

✉ Loretánské náměstí, Praha 1

☎ 2451 0780

🕐 Tue–Sun 9–noon, 1–4:30

🍴 None   🚇 None

🚌 22

🚊 None   ♿ None

✋ Moderate

↔ Strahovský klášter (➤ 24)

5
Pražský Hrad
(Prague Castle)

Dominating Hradčany with majestic assurance, Prague Castle has a history stretching back more than a thousand years and is still the Czech State's administrative centre.

The Castle's château-like appearance dates from 1753–75, when the Empress of Austria, Maria-Theresa, ordered its reconstruction, but the Gothic towers and spires of St Vitus's Cathedral are clues to a much older history. Sieges, burnings, floods and other misfortunes all took their toll on the churches and palaces, culminating in a disastrous fire in 1541 which engulfed the whole of Hradčany. Architecturally this was a blessing in disguise: the extensive repairs and restoration work which went on for more than a century, under the supervision of Italian and native architects, resulted in the stunning Renaissance and baroque interiors of today's Royal Palace.

Entry to the Castle is through a series of enclosed courtyards. In the first, the changing of the guard takes place hourly in the shadow of huge baroque sculptures of battling Titans (the soldiers' uniforms were designed by Theodor Pišt, who fitted out the actors in the film *Amadeus*). The entrance to the second courtyard is through the Matthias Gate, which dates from 1614. Directly opposite is the 19th-century Chapel of the Cross, now the Information Centre. On the other side of the courtyard, the Picture Gallery of Prague Castle contains paintings from the Imperial collections, including minor

works by Titian, Tintoretto, Veronese and Rubens. The third courtyard is dominated by St Vitus's Cathedral (➤ 18). To the right, the 18th-century façade of the Royal Palace conceals a network of halls and chambers on various levels, dating from the Romanesque period onwards. The centre-piece is the magnificent Vladislav Hall, built for King Vladislav Jagiello in the 1490s with Benedikt Ried's eye-catching rib-vaulted ceiling. Coronation feasts, political assemblies, even jousting competitions took place in the hall; knights on

horeseback entered by the Riders' Staircase at the far end. Off to the right are the former offices of the Chancellery of Bohemia, dating from the early 16th century, where, on 23 May 1618, after learning of the accession to the throne of the detested Archduke Ferdinand of Hapsburg, more than 100 Protestant noblemen burst into the far room and threw two Catholic governors and a secretary out of the window. The officials survived the fall but the incident, known as the Defenestration of Prague, marked the start of the Thirty Years' War. The Chapel of All Saints was redecorated in baroque style after the fire of 1541, but much more impressive is the Diet Hall, next door. Once a medieval parliament and later a throne room, it was designed by the Renaissance architect, Bonifaz Wohlmut, in 1563 and its walls are hung with portraits of the Hapsburgs. The Riders' Staircase leads down to the remains of the Romanesque and Gothic Palaces.

The Castle complex's other outstanding monument is St George's Basilica (➤ 43). A short walk away is the Lobkowicz Palace, reconstructed by Carlo Lurago in the 17th century. The impressive banqueting hall is open for concerts and recitals (other rooms are used by the Museum of Czech history). Two of the Castle's towers are open to visitors. Beyond Golden Lane, the Dalibor Tower was constructed in 1496 and is named after a nobleman imprisoned here on suspicion of complicity in a peasants' revolt. In the Mihulka, or Powder Tower, alchemists were once employed to elicit the secret of turning base metals into gold.

Above: *Ignaz Platzer's Fighting Giants dwarf the sentries outside the First Courtyard of Pražský hrad*

Below: *looking across River Vltava to Prague Castle*

6
Staroměstská Radnice
(Old Town Hall)

The star attraction of Prague's most famous landmark is the enchanting Astronomical Clock.

The Old Town Hall is actually a row of houses, adapted by the council over the centuries. In 1338 the burghers enlarged the merchant Volflin's house, and the adjoining tower and chapel were added in 1381. All that remains of the original façade is the door, with superb wood carvings by Matthias Rejsek. Neighbouring Křiž House was acquired six years later – the Rennaisance window, inscribed *Praga caput regni* (Prague, capital of the kingdom), is 16th-century. The house of furrier Mikš was added in 1548 and the house At the Cock in the 19th century.

The delicate mechanisms of the Astronomical Clock contrive to give the time of day, the months and seasons of the year, the signs of the zodiac, the course of the sun and the holidays of the Christian calendar. On the stroke of the hour, death, in the form of a skeleton, tolls a bell before making way for the 12 Apostles. When the cock crows and the clock chimes, other figures appear, including an infidel Turk and a preening Vanity.

Part of the Town Hall is open to the public. The council chamber has a fine casetto ceiling (1470). The oriel chapel, designed by Petr Parléř, also has a magnificent ceiling, painted with frescos of the four evangelists against an azure blue background with golden stars. Climb the tower for unsurpassed views across the red rooftops of the city.

✝ 31C2

✉ Staroměstská náměstí, Praha 1

☎ 2448 1111/2448 2751

🕐 Apr–Sep daily 9–6, Oct–Mar Mon 11–5, Tue–Sun 9–5. Closed 1 Jan, Easter Mon, 1 and 8 May, 5 and 6 July, 28 Oct, 24–6 Dec

🍴 Cafés (££), restaurants (£££) near by

Ⓜ Staroměstská

🚌 17

♿ Few

✋ Moderate

↔ Celetná (▶ 34), Dům U Kamenného Zvonu (▶ 38), Kostel Panny Marie před Týnem (▶ 46), Kostel Sv Mikuláše (▶ 48), Muzeum Českého Skla (▶ 55), Staroměstská náměstí (▶ 68)

❓ Guided tours available

The Astronomical Clock is one of the most appealing attractions in Staroměstské náměstí (Old Town Square)

7

Šternberský Palác
(Sternberg Palace)

The 17th-century baroque palace, built for Count Wenceslas Sternberg in 1698–1707, now houses the National Gallery's impressive collection of Old Masters.

The palace is set back from Hradčany Square (▶ 40): access is through the left-hand entrance of the Archbishop's Palace. The exhibition is arranged chronologically by the artists' country of origin. The gallery's proudest possession is Albrecht Dürer's scintillating *Feast of the Rose Garlands* (1506), acquired by Emperor Rudolph II because it features one of his ancestors, Maximilian I (shown in the foreground with Pope Julius II). German painting is also represented by Holbein the Elder and Lucas Cranach, including a charming *Adam and Eve*. Perhaps the gallery's strongest suit is Flemish and Dutch art of the 15th–17th centuries. There are works by Geertgen tot Sint Jans, Jan Gossaert and the Brueghels, father and son. Pieter Brueghel the Elder's animated calendar painting, *The Haymaking*, has a rhythmic, almost dance-like quality. Outstanding among the later work is a portrait by Rembrandt, *Scholar in his Study* (1634), and several paintings by Rubens, including *Martyrdom of St Thomas* (1637–9), which was commissioned for the church in Malá Strana. By comparison, the Italian Renaissance is less well represented, although Andrea della Robbia, Sebastiano del Piombo and Pietro della Francesca all feature in the collection and there are some fine altar

panels by the 14th-century Sienese artist, Pietro Lorenzetti. Paintings by artists of the 18th-century Venetian school, including Tiepolo and Canaletto, and two fine Spanish works, El Greco's *Head of Christ* and a portrait by Goya of Don Miguel de Lardizabal, can also be found in the gallery. The superb collection of 19th- and 20th-century French art is now in the Veletrzny Palace (▶ 26).

Albrecht Dürer's Feast of the Rose Garlands

✠ 40B2

✉ Hradčanské náměstí 15, Praha 1

☎ 2051 4634/7

🕓 Tue–Sun 10–6

🍴 None

🚇 None

🚌 22

🚊 None

♿ None

✋ Moderate

↔ Pražský hrad (▶ 20–1), Vojenské muzeum (▶ 72)

8

Strahovský Klášter
(Strahov Monastery)

The frescos in the Theological Hall were painted by Siard Nosecky, a canon of Strahov

Strahovní means 'watching over', and this ancient religious foundation, famous as a centre of learning, has been guarding the western approaches to Hradčany since the 12th century.

✚ 30A2

✉ Strahovské nádvoří, Hradčany

☎ 2451 0355

🕐 Tue–Sun 9–12, 12:30–5

🍴 Restaurant (££)

Ⓜ None

🚌 22

🅿 None

♿ Good

✋ Moderate

↔ Loreta (➤ 19),
Petřinské sady (➤ 64)

Above the baroque gateway is a statue of the founder of the Premonstratensian Order, St Norbert; to the left of the gate is the Church of St Roch, patron saint of plague victims, commissioned by Rudolf II in 1603 after Prague had narrowly escaped an epidemic. It is now used for modern art exhibitions. The twin-towered Abbey Church of the Nativity has a Romanesque core, but its present appearance dates from around 1750, when Anselmo Lurago remodelled the western façade. Mozart played the organ here on two occasions. The vaulted ceiling is sumptuously decorated with cartouches and frescos by Jiří Neunhertz, depicting the legend of St Norbert, whose remains were brought here from Magdeburg in 1627 and reburied in the chapel of St Ursula, on the left of the nave.

The library of the Strahov Monastery is more than 800 years old and among the finest in Europe. The Theological Hall, built in 1671–9 by Giovanni Orsi, has walls lined with elaborately carved bookcases, stacked with precious volumes and manuscripts. The Philosophical Hall dates from 1782–4, and its entire ceiling is covered with a delightful composition entitled *The Spiritual Development of Mankind*, by Franz Maulbertsch. The library contains over 130,000 volumes, including 2,500 books published before 1500, and 3,000 manuscripts. The oldest book, the 9th-century *Strahov Gospels*, is on show in the entrance.

9
Václavské náměstí
(Wenceslas Square)

*Wenceslas Square really comes alive after dark,
when its restaurants, cinemas and nightclubs
attract a boisterous crowd.*

Prague's most famous thoroughfare is actually an
impressive 750m-long boulevard, dominated at the
northern end by Josef Schulz's neo-Renaissance National
Museum (➤ 59). Once a horse market, Wenceslas Square
is better known today as a focus for political demonstration. When the Soviet army occupied Prague in August
1968 it was here that the distraught population gathered to
protest. Several months later a student, Jan Palach,
burned himself to death on the steps of the
National Museum. Following the collapse of
the Communist regime in December 1989,
Václav Havel and Alexander Dubček
appeared on the balcony of No 36 to greet
their ecstatic supporters. Palach and other
victims of the regime are commemorated in
a small shrine in front of Josef Myslbek's
equestrian statue of St Wenceslas, which
was unveiled in 1912.

Wenceslas Square became a show-case
for modern Czech architecture when
the traditional two- and three-
storey baroque houses were
demolished in the 19th
century. The neo-Renaissance
Wiehl House was completed in
1896 and is decorated with florid
sgraffito and statuary by Mikuláš
Aleš. Many of the sumptuous art
nouveau interiors and fittings in
the Europa Hotel (No 25) have
survived and are also worth investigating. The functionalist Koruna palác
(No 1), a covered shopping arcade
with a stunning glass dome dating
from 1911, became the model for
other passageways linking the
square with the neighbouring
streets (the Lucerna, at No 61, was
built by Václav Havel's grandfather).
The former insurance offices on the
corner of Jindřišská could well have
been the stuff of nightmares for
Franz Kafka when he worked here
as a clerk in 1906–7.

➕ 31C2

✉ Václavské náměstí,
Praha 1

🍴 Cafés (£), restaurants
(££–£££)

🚇 Můstek, Muzeum

🚌 3, 9, 14, 24

🚆 None   ♿ Few

✋ Free

↔ Na Příkopě (➤ 58),
Národní muzeum
(➤ 59)

*An equestrian statue of
St Wenceslas presides
over the square that
bears his name*

10
Veletržní Palác
(Veletrzny Palace)

The gallery's outstanding collection of modern Czech and European art is housed in a 1920s constructivist palace.

✛ 31D3

✉ Dukelskych hrdinů 47, Praha 7

☎ 2430 1024/1111

🕐 Tue–Wed, Fri–Sun 10–6, Thu 10–9

🍴 Café (££)

Ⓜ Vltavská

🚊 5, 12, 17

🚌 Holešovice

♿ Few

✋ Moderate

↔ Lapidárium (➤ 51)

Designed by Oldřich Tyl and Josef Fuchs for the Prague Trade Fair of 1928, the enormous glass-fronted building was described by the famous modernist architect, Le Corbusier, as 'breathtaking'. The priceless French collection runs the gamut of Impressionist and Post-Impressionist artists. Among the highlights are *Two Women among the Flowers* (1875), by Monet, *Green Rye*, by Van Gogh (1889), and one of Gauguin's Tahiti paintings, *Flight* (1902). Picasso is represented by several contrasting paintings, ranging from an arresting, primitivist *Self Portrait*, dating from 1907, to *Clarinet* (1911), a classic example of analytic Cubism. There are also works by Braque, Chagall, Derain, Vlaminck, Raoul Dufy, Fernand Léger, Albert Marquet and Marie Laurencin. Among the sculptures are works by Rodin, Henri Laurens, and an unusual study of a dancer by Dégas.

Two Women among the Flowers *(1875) by Monet, part of the gallery's outstanding French collection*

French painting was a major source of inspiration for Czech artists seeking an alternative to the predominant German culture of the late 19th century. Jan Zrzavy, Bohumil Kubišta and Emil Filla all progressed from neo-Impressionism to more abstract styles. Kubišta's *Still Life with Funnel* (1910) was directly influenced by a similar study by Picasso. Other artists producing Cubist works at the time include Filla, Václav Špála and the sculptor Otto Gutfreund. The Czechs' affinity with French art becomes even more noticeable in the inter-war period, when the two countries were closely bound together by political and diplomatic ties. The crowning moment came in 1935, when the founder of the Surrealist movement, André Breton, visited Czechoslovakia at the invitation of the Prague Surrealists, Jindřich Štyrský, Vincenc Makovsky and Toyen (Marie Čermínová). The exhibition concludes with sections on post-war and contemporary art.

What To See

Above: *mosaic on an upper facade in Staroměstské náměstí*
Right: *warrior in medieval costume at Melnik*

27

Prague

The view from the Charles Bridge at dusk: in the foreground, a procession of dramatic sculptures recedes into the distance; assembled behind them an extraordinary composition of gilded crosses, tented Gothic towers and baroque domes is silhouetted against the sunset. This is Prague in a nutshell. The city's extraordinary charms lie in the painstaking detail of its architecture – a gabled roof, an ornate railing, a sculpted house sign, a pair of Atlantes supporting a portal, a votive statue ensconced in a niche, a street lamp decorated with dancing maidens. Wherever one turns there is some magic to catch the eye.

' Prague always had two faces. She was officially German and unofficially Czech. Or she was officially Czech, but unofficially she had within herself a German city… She was officially Austrian and unofficially anti–Austrian. She was officially Catholic and unofficially anti–Christian. '

WILLY LORENZ
To Bohemia with Love

Prague

Prague is best enjoyed at a leisurely pace. It's a compact city: the main sights are easily accessible on foot, and much of the central area is traffic free, with cafés and pubs on almost every street corner.

For sightseeing purposes, Prague falls naturally into its four medieval divisions: Hradčany (the area around the castle), Malá Strana (Lesser Quarter), Staré Město (Old Town) and Nové Město (New Town).

Hradčany is dominated by Prague Castle, primarily a tourist attraction with its cathedral, museums and galleries, but also a seat of government – the President and his ministers have their offices here.

Malá Strana, on the slopes beneath the castle, is distinguished by the green of its gardens and orchards, created in the 17th century by the aristocrats who built their palaces here. Crowning Malostranské náměstí is the majestic, green-domed Church of St Nicholas. Nearer the Vltava, the secluded neighbourhood of Na Kampě is perfect for a romantic evening stroll.

Beyond the Charles Bridge is Staré Město, historically the most important of the four towns. It grew up around Staroměstské náměstí, still a popular meeting place and one of the prettiest squares in Europe. The maze of narrow streets and arcaded courtyards conceals gabled houses, brightly painted shop fronts, churches and taverns.

The New Town – actually founded in the 14th century – is the commercial and administrative heart of the city. Even first-time visitors will probably have heard of Wenceslas Square (Václavské náměstí). 'Square' is actually a misnomer – it's really a long boulevard, lined with shops, hotels and nightclubs, that really comes alive after dark.

View towards Kostel Panny Marie před Týnem (Týn Church), one of many superb vistas to be enjoyed from the tower of Staroměstská radnice (Old Town Hall)

29

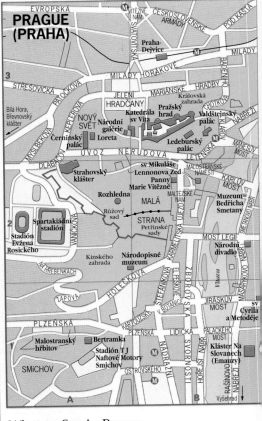

What to See in Prague

ANEŽSKÝ KLÁŠTER
(ST AGNES CONVENT)

✪✪✪

One of Prague's loveliest relgious buildings, the convent was founded in 1234 by Agnes, sister of King Wenceslas I. St Agnes introduced the Order of Poor Clares into Bohemia and was the first abbess. Completed by the end of the 14th century and sacked by the Hussites in the 15th, the convent was eventually dissolved in 1782. Restoration work has only recently been completed. The most impressive building is the Church of the Holy Saviour, an outstanding example of early Gothic architecture. Note the capitals which are decorated with reliefs showing rulers of the Přemyslid dynasty. During the restoration the burial place of some of these kings and queens was unearthed, including the tomb of King

✚ 31C3
✉ U Milosrdnych 17, Praha 1
☎ 2481 0628
🕐 Tue–Sun 10–6
🍴 Restaurant (££)
Ⓜ Staroměstská
🚌 5, 17, 14, 26
♿ Few
Moderate
↔ Josefov (➤ 17)

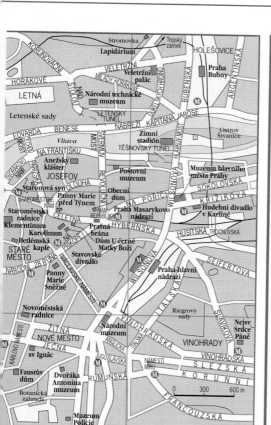

The timeless cloisters of Anežský klášter. The Gothic vaulting dates from the 14th century

Wenceslas in the Church of St Francis (which is now used as a concert venue).

The convent is a branch of the National Gallery and contains an exhibition of 19th-century Czech painting, mainly landscapes and portraits although there are some evocative scenes of turn-of-the-century Prague. The leading artist of the period, Josef Mánes, is well represented. Other artists who feature here include Mikuláš Aleš, the sculptor Josef Myslbek, Karel Postl, Antonín Machek, Josef Navrátil and Julius Mařák.

*This room in the Mozart
Museum is decorated in
18th-century style*

BERTRAMKA (MOZART MUSEUM) ✪✪✪

This hillside villa, the home of the soprano, Josefina
Dušek, and her composer husband František, was where
Wolfgang Amadeus Mozart stayed on his visits to Prague
in 1787 and 1791. Although the house was badly damaged
by fire in 1873, the rooms Mozart occupied have survived
and now contain a small exhibition on the composer and
his happy relationship with the Bohemian capital. The most
highly valued items, apart from the manuscripts, are his
harpsichord and a lock of his hair. But his presence can
best be felt in the lovely garden. It was here, on the night
of 28 October 1787, that Mozart dashed off the sublime
overture to his opera, *Don Giovanni*, just one night before
the première was given in the Estates Theatre (➤ 70).

BETLÉMSKÁ KAPLE (BETHLEHEM CHAPEL) ✪

The Bethlehem Chapel was built by followers of the radical
preacher Jan Milíč of Kroměříž in 1391–4. In 1402 a
lecturer at the university, Jan Hus, was appointed Rector
and drew huge crowds to his sermons, which were given
in Czech, rather than Latin. Hus was a charismatic figure,
but his attacks on the wealth and corruption of the Catholic
hierarchy did not endear him to his religious superiors. He
eventually overstepped the bounds of orthodoxy, arguing
that the Pope had no authority over the Bohemian Church
and that doctrine should be based on the scriptures alone.
Hus was excommunicated in 1412 and the Bethlehem
Chapel was closed. Summoned to defend his teachings at
the Council of Constance two years later, Hus consented
to leave the safe territory of Prague only after being issued
with a guarantee of safe conduct by the Emperor
Sigismund. But the Emperor went back on his word: Hus

was arrested, condemned as a heretic and, on 6 July 1415, burnt at the stake.

The decision to reconstruct the Chapel was taken in 1949. The prayer hall is trapezoid in form, the timber roof resting on plain stone supports. The total area measures 798sq m – ample space for the congregations of 3,000 who came to hear Hus speak. Painted on the walls are scenes from the life of the reformer and his followers, based on contemporary sources and painted by members of the Czech Academy of Fine Arts. Upstairs in the former preacher's house is an exhibition: 'The Bethlehem Chapel in Czech history and the tradition of non-Catholic thinking'.

A mural of the Annunciation painted on a gable in Betlémské náměstí (Bethelem Square): art bestows individuality on many of the buildings in Prague

BÍLÁ HORA (WHITE MOUNTAIN) ✪

In the space of an hour, on 8 November 1620, the Catholic Hapsburg army, under Maximilian of Bavaria, routed the Czech Protestants on this hillock outside Prague, deciding the fate of Bohemia for the next 300 years. The battle is commemorated by a small stone monument and the Church of Our Lady of Victories (1704–14).

Also in the park is the unusual Renaissance hunting lodge Letohrádek Hvĕdza (Star Castle), built in 1555–7. The six-pointed plan was the notion of its original owner, Ferdinand of Tyrol, son of the Governor of Bohemia. The castle now contains exhibitions devoted to the work of the writer Alois Jirásek and the painter, Mikoláš Aleš.

✚ Off map 30A3
✉ Vypich
☎ Castle: 367 938
🕒 Castle: Tue–Sat 10–4, Sun 10–5
🚌 8, 22
♿ None
🎫 Castle: cheap
🔁 Břevnovský klášter (➤ 34)

The stunning ceiling frescos in Břevnovský klášter have only recently been restored. They date from the 18th century

BŘEVNOVSKÝ KLÁŠTER (BŘEVNOV MONASTERY) ✪✪

There has been a monastery in Břevnov since AD 993 although the present baroque complex, designed by Christoph and Karl Dientzenhofer, dates from 1708–45. Recently the monastery was returned to the Benedictines and the restored buildings are being opened to the public. The remarkable St Margaret's Church, built over a Romanesque crypt, has breathtaking oval ceiling frescos by Johann Steinfels depicting scenes from the legend of St Adalbert, while the Theresian Hall has a magnificent painting of Blessed Günther by Kosmas Assam.

CELETNÁ ✪

The street of bakers is one of the oldest in the city and was on the royal processional route. Its handsomely decorated baroque façades conceal in many cases Romanesque or Gothic foundations. An exception is the Cubist House of the Black Madonna (➤ 38). The house at No 36, with the wrought-iron balcony supported by Atlantes, is the former mint. Some of Prague's best known restaurants are on Celetná: House At the Golden Vulture (No 22), At the Spider (No 17) and At the Golden Stag (No 11). Celetná is also a good place to shop for glassware, jewellery and antiques.

ČERNÍNSKÝ PALÁC (ČERNÍN PALACE) ✪

So much stone was used in the construction of this vast palace, with a façade stretching the entire length of Loretánské náměstí (135m), that it was said that the builders were being paid by the cubic metre. Certainly the palace's original owner, Count Jan Černín of Chudenice, Imperial Ambassador to Venice, spared no expense on the interior decoration – the work of the sculptor, Matyás Braun and the painter, Vaclav Reiner, among others. In 1948, 20 years after the palace was acquired by the Ministry of Foreign Affairs, Jan Masaryk, son of the founder of Czechoslovakia and the only non-Communist member of the government, fell to his death from an upper floor window into the courtyard below. It is now widely believed that Masaryk was murdered on the orders of Stalin.

- 30A3
- Loretánské náměstí, Praha 1
- 2418 1111
- Not open to public
- 22
- None
- Loreta (► 19), Strahovský klášter (► 24)

The stupendous façade of the 17th-century Černínský palác dominates the western end of Hradčany

CHRÁM PANNY MARIE SNĚŽNÉ (OUR LADY OF THE SNOWS) ✪

Founded in 1347 by Charles IV, Our Lady of the Snows was to have been the largest church in Prague – 40m high and 110m long – but the outbreak of the Hussite wars interrupted work on the building. In 1603 the completed choir was restored to the Franciscans and given a baroque facelift as well as a new vaulted ceiling. Otherwise, all that remains of the 14th-century church are the crumbling pediment over the north gateway and the pewter font. The Franciscan Gardens near the south wall were originally part of the monastery grounds and are now a public park.

- 31C2
- Jungmannovo náměstí 18, Praha 1
- 265 742
- Daily 7AM–7:30PM
- Můstek
- Few
- Free
- Václavské náměstí (► 25)

CHRÁM SVATÉHO MIKULÁŠ (► 16 TOP TEN)

Food & Drink

You can be sure of one thing when you eat out in Prague – or anywhere else in the Czech Republic, for that matter: you will not go hungry. All the national dishes are incredibly rich and filling, and portions are gargantuan.

Meat and Veg

Pork is still a staple of the traditional Czech meal

Czech cuisine is heavily meat-based. Pork, beef and chicken are all standard fare – but the pig is king. Popular dishes include pork with dumplings and *sauerkraut* (pickled cabbage), roast duck with bacon dumplings, and roast beef with a sour cream sauce. *Wiener schnitzel*, known to the Czechs as *smažený řízek*, is another favourite. In expensive restaurants, you're likely to encounter game – venison, pheasant, hare or even wild boar. Most meat is boiled or roasted and served swimming in gravy and accompanied by potatoes or dumplings (*knedlíky*).

Fresh vegetables, other than the ubiquitous *sauerkraut*, are appearing on menus with increasing frequency and you'll usually be able to order a side salad of tomato and onions, cucumber or just plain lettuce. Some restaurants even serve noodles or pasta as an accompaniment to standard Czech items. But vegetarians should note that

many apparently meatless dishes are cooked in animal fat. The best advice is to declare yourself at the outset: *Jsem vegetarian (-ka* for the feminine form).

Of the fish dishes, boiled carp served in melted butter, roasted pike, fillet of trout cooked in a green pepper sauce and smoked salmon are all delicious. Try to leave some room for dessert, but don't count the calories. Pancakes may be filled with ice cream, jam or stewed fruit. Apple strudel and plum dumplings are reliable stand-bys.

Beer

Czech beer is justifiably famous and is fully appreciated by the Czechs themselves – the Republic boasts the highest *per capita* consumption in the world: 153.6 litres annually. Plzeň produces the clear golden nectar known as Pilsner Urquell in Germany and locally as Plzeňský Prazdroj. Gambrinus is another common brand. The other main centre of beer production is the southern Bohemian town of České Budějovice, Budweis in German. Don't be misled by the name – the American beer, Budweiser, and the Czech brew, Budvar, have nothing in common. All these brews are delicious, but local Prague beers like Staropramen and Braník are just as good. If you fancy trying a dark (*tmave*) beer, head for the famous pub known as U Fleků, which produces its own brand. The generic term for beer is *pivo*.

Wines and Spirits

Most Czech wine is produced in the warmer, more sheltered parts of southern Moravia and is consumed locally, rather than exported. The best of the red wines is Frankovka or Vavřinecké – Tramín is a reliable white variety. The Mělník region, just north of Prague, produces a small amount of wine of variable quality (sometimes none at all, if the weather is bad). A dry white wine known as Rulandské bílé is probably the best, and can often be found on menus. There are three types of liqueur worth sampling: Borovicka, a fiery, juniper-flavoured spirit with the impact of an Italian grappa, which should be treated with the same respect; Slivovice, a plum brandy and, best of all, the wonderfully aromatic Becherovka, a herb-based drink concocted in the spa town of Karlovy Vary.

Czech beer is renowned throughout the world. Pilsner lager was first brewed in Plzeň in 1842

🔲 31C2
✉ Řetězová 222/3, Praha 1
🕐 May–Sep Tue–Sun 10–6.
Closed 1 Jan, Easter
Mon, 1, 8 May, 5, 6 July,
28 Oct, 24–6 Dec
🚇 Národní třída
🚌 6, 9, 18, 22
💰 Moderate
↔ Betlémská kaple (➤ 32),
Karlův most (➤ 40),
Klementinum (➤ 44)

🔲 31C2
✉ Celetná 34, Praha 1
☎ 2421 1732
🕐 Tue–Sat 10–6. Closed 1
Jan, Easter Mon, 1 and 8
May, 5 and 6 July, 28
Oct, 24–6 Dec
🍴 Cafés (££), restaurants
(£££)
🚇 Náměstí Republiky
♿ None
💰 Moderate
↔ Celetná (➤ 34), Prašná
brána (➤ 66)

The famous statue of the Black Madonna that gives the house on Celetná its name

🔲 31C2
✉ Staroměstská náměstí 13, Praha 1
☎ 2482 7526
🕐 Tue–Sun 10–6. Closed 1
Jan, Easter Mon, 1, 8
May, 5, 6 July, 28 Oct,
24–6 Dec
🚇 Staroměstská
💰 Cheap
↔ Celetná (➤ 34), Kostel
Panny Marie před Týnem
(➤ 46), Kostel Svatého
Mikuláše (➤ 48)

DŮM PÁNŮ Z KUNŠTÁTU A PODĚBRAD   ⭐⭐
(HOUSE OF THE LORDS KUNSTAT AND PODEBRAD)

The medieval chambers of this former palace, with original Romanesque cross-vaulted ceilings and fireplaces, are now open to the public. Dating from about 1200, they once formed the ground floor of a building which was enlarged in the 15th century for the Lords of Kunstat and Poděbrady. There is a small exhibition on its most famous resident, George of Podebrad, who became King of Bohemia in 1457.

DŮM U ČERNÉ MATKY BOŽÍ   ⭐⭐
(HOUSE OF THE BLACK MADONNA)

While Cubist painting is common in Europe, Cubist architecture is unique to Bohemia. Designed by Josef Gočár in 1911–12, this innovative building was right at the cutting edge of the modernist movement, with its façades broken into multiple planes in order to create an unusual interplay of light and shade. Behind a grille on the first floor is the statue of the Black Mother of God, which gives the building its name.

Inside is a permanent exhibition on Czech Cubism 1911–19.

DŮM U KAMENNÉHO ZVONU   ⭐⭐
(HOUSE AT THE STONE BELL)

This magnificent Gothic tower with its characteristic hipped roof was built as a palace for King John of Luxembourg around 1340. The sculpted decoration of the west façade was rediscovered in the 1960s, having long been concealed by a rococo facelift. Make sure you don't overlook the stone bell on the corner of the building which gives the house its name. Concerts and exhibitions are now held here and visitors can see original Gothic features, including extensive fragments of medieval wall painting. The ceiling beams, delicately painted with floral motifs, date from the reign of Charles IV.

DVOŘÁKA ANTONÍNA MUZEUM (DVORAK MUSEUM) ✪

This beautiful baroque mansion, built by Kilian Dientzenhofer in 1717–20 for a prominant Czech nobleman, acquired its present name, Villa Amerika, in the 19th century – there was an eating house of that name near by. It is therefore entirely appropriate that the building now honours the composer of the 'New World' symphony, Antonín Dvořák (1841–1904).

Unfortunately, the palatial interior, with partly restored frescos by Johann Schlor, is not really suitable for such an intimate exhibition, especially given the composer's decidedly modest background and lifestyle. (His apartment on Žitná Street, not far from here, was demolished long ago.) The exhibits, spread over two floors, include autographed scores, photographs, busts and portraits, correspondence with fellow musicians (the composers, Brahms and Tchaikovsky, and the German conductor, Hans von Bülow, were among Dvořák's friends and admirers) and a number of personal effects including his viola, Bible and spectacles. The first floor is also used for concerts.

🚩 31C1
✉ Ke Karlovu 20, Praha 2
☎ 298 214
🕐 Tue–Sun 10–5
Ⓜ IP Pavlova
🚌 272 ♿ Few
🍴 Cheap
↔ Muzeum Policie (➤ 56)

Above: the Czech composer Antonín Dvořák's piano, one of the exhibits on display in the Villa Amerika

EXPOZICE FRANZE KAFKY (FRANZ KAFKA EXHIBITION) ✪

A sculpted relief marks the site of the house where Franz Kafka was born in 1883. Only the doorway of the original building, 'At the Tower', remains following a fire in 1887. There is a photographic exhibition of Kafka's life on the ground floor.

Left: this arresting sculpture by Karel Hladík marks the site of Franz Kafka's birthplace

🚩 31C2
✉ U Radnice 5, Praha 1
☎ None
🕐 Tue–Fri 10–6, Sat 10–5
🍴 Café (£), restaurants (££–£££) near by
Ⓜ Staroměstská
🍴 Cheap
↔ Celetná (➤ 34), Dům U Kamenného Zvonu (➤ 38), Kostel Panny Marie před Týnem (➤ 46), Kostel Svatého Mikuláše (➤ 48), Muzeum Českého Skla (➤ 55), Staroměstská náměstí (➤ 68)

Did you know ?

'Prague does not let go...This little mother has claws', Franz Kafka once confided to his diary. His love-hate relationship with the city is reflected in the novels The Trial and The Castle, where Prague's menacing presence looms over the characters.

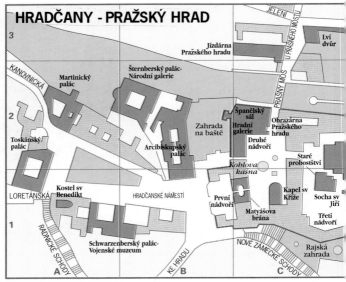

HRADČANSKÉ NÁMĚSTÍ (HRADČANY SQUARE) ✪

This is a square of stunning Renaissance and baroque façades. The Archbishop's Palace (No 16) was given its eye-catching rococo facelift in 1764 by the architect Johan Wirch, and is adorned with the family crest of the original owner, Archbishop Antonín Příchovský. Across the square is the Renaissance Schwarzenberg Palace. The yellow-fronted Tuscany Palace (No 5), once owned by the Duke of Tuscany (whose coat of arms is emblazoned above the portal) dates from 1689–91. Jaroslav Bořita of Martinitz, one of the defenestrated ministers of 1618, gave his name to the handsome palace at No 8 with its figurative sgraffito illustrating the story of Joseph and Potiphar and other biblical tales.

JOSEFOV (➤ 17 TOP TEN)

KARLŮV MOST (CHARLES BRIDGE) ✪✪✪

This remarkable sandstone bridge, designed in 1357 by Petr Parléř for King Charles IV, links the Old Town with the Lesser Quarter. In 1657 a bronze crucifix with a Hebrew inscription was erected on the bridge – the only ornament at that time. The idea caught on and now more than 30 sculptures adorn the parapets. Perhaps the finest of them, by Matthias Braun (1710), shows St Luitgard kissing Christ's wounds in a vision. The figure with the starry halo is St John of Nepomuk whose tortured body was hurled

Sidebar (left column):

40B1
Hradcanské náměstí, Praha 1
Café (£)
22
Few
Pražský hrad (➤ 20–1)

Right: *street musicians entertaining the tourists in Hradčany*

30B2
Karlův most, Praha 1
Daily; towers: 10–6 (Oct–May 10–5)
Staroměstská
12, 22 Good
Towers: cheap
Klementinum (➤ 44), Křižovnické náměstí (➤ 50)

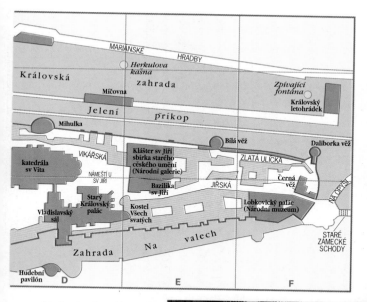

into the river from this spot in 1393 after he had dared to side with his archbishop against the king. The Old Town Bridge Tower was built by Petr Parléř in 1391. The sculptures above the arch show St Vitus in the company of Kings Wenceslas IV and Charles IV – the views from the gallery are spectacular. Today the Charles Bridge is made all the more colourful by the buskers and street traders who have made it their own in recent years.

KAROLINUM ✪

Founded in 1348 by Charles IV, the Karolinum is the oldest university in Central Europe. It acquired the house of the former mint master, Johlin Rothlev of Kutna Hora, in 1383 (until then classes had been held in churches or private houses). Although Rothlev's house was completely remodelled in the 18th century by František Kaňka, the exquisite oriel window protruding from the façade on Ovocny trh is a reminder of its medieval origins. The Karolinum has long outgrown its original premises, which are currently occupied by the university Rectorate.

➕ 31C2
✉ Železná 9, Praha 1
☎ 2422 8600
Ⓜ Můstek
♿ None
🔄 Celetná (➤ 34), Staroměstské náměstí (➤ 68), Stavovské divadlo (➤ 70)

For nearly 700 years the Karlův most (Charles Bridge) has been the main link between Staré Město (the Old Town) and Mala Straná (the Lesser Quarter)

KATEDRÁLA SVATÉHO VÍTA (► 18 TOP TEN)

KLÁŠTER SVATÉHO JIŘÍ
(ST GEORGE'S CONVENT AND BASILICA)

✪✪✪

St George's Convent houses the National Gallery's collection of Czech Gothic and baroque art (see below), and adjoining it is the Basilica, one of the oldest religious foundations in Prague, dating back to 920 and reconstructed in its present Romanesque form after a fire in 1142 (the baroque façade is a 17th-century addition). To the right of the entrance to the crypt is the painted wooden tomb of the founder, Prince Vratislav. Climb the ornate stairway for a good view of the faded 13th-century frescos, depicting the Heavenly Jerusalem, in the apse, and of the equally striking Renaissance paintings in the Chapel of St Ludmilla.

Some of the original altar panels from the Basilica have been preserved in the Convent next door, which has an exceptionally rich collection of religious painting and sculpture from the 14th century, widely regarded as the golden age of Bohemian art. Look out for two artists active in the reign of Charles IV: the Master of the Vyšší Brod Altar and Master Theodoric, whose lustrous portraits of the saints were intended for the chapel of Karlštejn Castle. The carved wooden sculptures come from churches all over Bohemia and convey an astonishing range of emotions, from the despairing anguish of the Jedlka Pietà to the maternal playfulness of the Krumlov Madonna, while the crucifixion tableaux have a dramatic intensity reminiscent of a medieval mystery play.

The collection of baroque painting features artists such as Karel Škréta, Petr Brandl and Jan Kupecky, and the sculptors Matthias Braun, Ferdinand Brokoff and Ignaz Platzer.

➕ 41E2
✉ Jiřské námsětí 33, Hradčany
☎ 5732 0536
🕐 Tue–Sun 10–6
🍴 Café (£), restaurants (££–£££) near by
🚌 22   ♿ Few
💰 Moderate
↔ Pražský hrad (► 20–1), Zlatá ulička (► 73)

The Romanesque Basilica dates from 1142

31C3

U Starého hřbitova 3a, Praha 1

2481 0099

Sun–Fri 9–4:30. Closed Jewish hols

Staroměstská

17, 18

Few

Moderate

Obřadní síň (► 64), Stary židovský hřbitov (► 69)

KLAUSOVÁ SYNAGÓGA (KLAUSEN SYNAGOGUE) ✪

A number of religious schools and other buildings known as *klausen* were cleared away after the great fire of 1689 to make way for this early baroque synagogue. The fine interior, with barrel-vaulted roof, stuccoed ceiling ornamentation and stained-glass windows, has been restored and now contains an exhibition on local Jewish customs and traditions, including old Hebrew manuscripts and prints, beautifully worked Torah ornaments, skull caps embroidered in satin and velvet, bronze Hanukkah lamps and a curious wooden alms box (c1800) with a supplicating hand and arm. The marble Holy Ark, made in 1696 at the expense of Samuel Openheim, has also been restored.

31C2

Mariánské náměstí 5, Praha 1

2166 3111

Restricted times

Staroměstská

17, 18   Few

Karlův most (► 40), Křižovnické náměstí (► 50)

The magnificent Baroque Hall of the Klementinum is now part of the National Library

KLEMENTINUM

When the Emperor Ferdinand I invited the Jesuits to Prague in 1556 to spearhead the Counter-Reformation, they moved into the former monastery of St Clement. In the 17th century the Karolinum (► 41) merged with the Klementinum, giving them a monopoly of higher education, and they undertook a building programme which lasted over 150 years. The walls of the baroque fortress enclosed a college, schools, churches, a library, a theatre, an observatory and a printing shop. When the Jesuit Order was dissolved in 1773 the complex was taken over by the university; today it belongs to the National Library. The Klementinum is being renovated, but buildings which may be open include the Church of St Saviour (1638–48), the Baroque Hall of the former Jesuit Library and the Chapel of Mirrors (1724–30, open for concerts).

A Walk Around Josefov

The area to the north of the Old Town, now known as Josefov, was first settled by Jews in the 13th century. Most of the surviving sights and monuments date from the 16th and 17th centuries.

Start in Maiselova, heading away from Old Town Square, and pass the Maisel Synagogue. At the crossroads, turn left onto Široká. On your right is the Pinkas Synagogue.

The Maisel Synagogue (➤ 53) has an exhibition of ceremonial silverware from Bohemia and Moravia. The Pinkas Synagogue (➤ 65) is now a memorial to Holocaust victims.

Leave by the back entrance of the Pinkas Synagogue, which leads into the Old Jewish Cemetery (➤ 69).

The oldest graves here date from the 15th century. At the opposite gate is the Ceremonial Hall and the Klausen Synagogue (➤ 44).

Walk east along Ust Hřbitova Červená to the junction with Maiselova.

On your right you will find the late baroque Town Hall, now the Jewish Community Centre, the High Synagogue and the 13th-century step-gabled Old-New Synagogue (➤ 69).

Continue along Ust Hřbitova Červená between the synagogues, then turn right onto Pařížská. Turn left at Široká and cross Dušní to Vňská.

Moorish-style motifs decorate the Spanish Synagogue (on the corner), which dates from 1867–8.

Distance
1km

Time
2hrs

Start/end point
Metro Staroměstská
🚇 31C2

Lunch
U Golema (££)
✉ Maiselova 8
☎ 232 8165

The grave of the renowned rabbi Jehuda Löw in the Starý židovský hřbitov (Old Jewish Cemetery). Visitors place pebbles on the tomb as a mark of respect

45

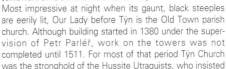

31C2

Staroměstské náměstí, Praha 1

231 8186

Services Mon–Fri 5:30PM, Sat 1PM, Sun 11:30AM, 9PM

Cafés (£), restaurants (£££) near by

Staroměstská

None

Free

Celetná (➤ 34), Dům U Kamenného Zvonu (➤ 38), Kostel Svatého Mikuláše (➤ 48), Muzeum Českého Skla (➤ 55), Staroměstské náměstí (➤ 68)

Golden statue of the Virgin between the towers of Kostel Panny Marie před Týnem

KOSTEL PANNY MARIE PŘED TÝNEM (CHURCH OF OUR LADY BEFORE TÝN) ✪✪

Most impressive at night when its gaunt, black steeples are eerily lit, Our Lady before Týn is the Old Town parish church. Although building started in 1380 under the supervision of Petr Parléř, work on the towers was not completed until 1511. For most of that period Týn Church was the stronghold of the Hussite Utraquists, who insisted on taking communion in both kinds (the symbolic gilded chalice which hung from the gable was melted down after the Counter-Reformation to make an effigy of the Virgin). The beautifully sculpted portal dates from 1390. The gloomy interior is an uneasy marriage of Gothic and baroque styles. Over the high altar are paintings by Karol Škréta, dating from 1640–60, while Gothic features include a *pietà*, a 15th-century pulpit and a pewter font (1414). In front of the high altar is the tomb of the Danish astronomer, Tycho Brahe (1546–1601).

30B1

Resslova

295 595

Tue–Sun 10–4

Karlovo náměstí

3, 4, 6, 14, 16, 18, 22, 24

None

Cheap

KOSTEL SVATÉHO CYRILA A METODÉJE (CHURCH OF SS CYRIL AND METHODIUS) ✪

A plaque on the bullet-scarred wall of this church commemorates the Free Czech paratroopers who died here on 18 June 1942, after taking part in the assassination of the Nazi Governor of Bohemia and Moravia, Reinhard Heydrich. Members of the Czech Orthodox community hid them in the crypt, but they were discovered, and committed suicide rather than fall into enemy hands. SS Cyril and Methodius has recently been designated a National Memorial to the victims of the Heydrich Terror.

30B2

Karmelitská, Praha 1

530 752 Daily 8:30–7

12, 22 Free

Malostranské náměstí (➤ 53)

KOSTEL PANNY MARIE VÍTĚZNÉ (OUR LADY VICTORIOUS) ✪

The chief attraction of this 17th-century church is a wax effigy of the infant Jesus, usually known by its Italian name Il Bambino di Praga. Believed to have miracle-working properties, the statue was brought from Spain in 1628 by

Polxena of Lobkowicz and presented to the Carmelite nuns, who continue to care for its 39 embroidered outfits.

KOSTEL SVATÉHO JAKUBA
(ST JAMES'S CHURCH)

The Minorite Order of Franciscans commissioned this baroque church in 1689 after its 13th-century predecessor had been destroyed in a fire. The paintings in the nave, galleries and 21 side altars are by a variety of artists, including Franz Voget, Petr Brandl and Václav Reiner, who also contributed the effulgent *Martyrdom of St James* over the high altar. Equally remarkable is the stunning tomb of the Chancellor of Bohemia, Count Vratislav of Mitrovice, on the left-hand side of the nave. It was sculpted in marble and sandstone by Ferdinand Brokof. A shrivelled arm which dangles just inside the door belonged to a jewel thief caught stealing here in the 16th century.

St James's is renowned for its musical tradition. A choir sings at high mass on Sundays, accompanied on the organ, a splendid baroque instrument dating from 1702. There are regular concerts and recitals here.

31C2

Malá Stupartská 6, Praha 1

Mon–Fri 7–5. Closed Sat,
Sun except for services

Můstek

None

Free

Celetná (➤ 34),
Staroměstské náměstí
(➤ 68)

31C2

Staroměstské náměstí, Praha 1

Tue–Fri, Sun 10–noon

Cafés (£), restaurants (££–£££) near by

Staroměstská

None   Free

Expozice Franz Kafka (► 39), Staroměstské náměstí (► 68)

KOSTEL SVATÉHO MIKULÁŠE (ST NICHOLAS'S CHURCH)   ✪✪

This beautifully proportioned baroque masterpiece was designed by the prolific Kilian Dientzenhofer in 1732 and completed three years later. (The sculptures of saints are by Antonin Braun.) St Nicholas stands on the site of a much older Gothic church. When, in the spirit of the Enlightenment, the Emperor Joseph II evicted the Benedictines later in the 18th century, on the grounds that they were not performing a useful function, the church was used as a warehouse and fell into disrepair. It was saved during World War I when the commander of the occupying garrison invited local artists to restore Kosmas Asam's frescos of SS Nicholas and Benedict in the dome. In other respects the building lacks the exuberance of baroque ornamentation.

Since 1920 St Nicholas has belonged to the Czech Reformed (Hussite) Church and is regularly used for concerts.

A baroque flourish on the door of Kostel Svatého Mikuláše

30B3

Letenská, Praha 1

530 218

Daily and for services

Cafés (£), restaurants (££) near by

Malostranská

12, 22

None

Free

Malostranské náměstí (► 53), Nerudova (► 60–1), Valdštejnský palác (► 71)

KOSTEL SVATÉHO TOMÁŠE (ST THOMAS'S CHURCH)   ✪✪

The spire of this attractive church rises impressively above the rooftops of Lesser Town Square. Founded in 1285, at the same time as the neighbouring Augustinian monastery, it has undergone many reincarnations over the centuries, the latest in 1723–31 when Kilian Dientzenhofer completely remodelled the Gothic church after it had been damaged by lightning. The interior is captivating, with glorious ceiling frescos by Václav Reiner depicting the life of St Augustine and, in the dome, the legend of St Thomas. Amazingly, he completed the work in just two years. Other distinguished artists, including Karel Škréta and the sculptor, Ferdinand Brokoff, also contributed to the décor, while the paintings (copies) over the high altar, of St Thomas and St Augustine, were commissioned from Rubens (the originals are now in the Šternberský Palác, ► 23).

A Walk Along the Royal Route

This walk follows the processional route taken by the kings and queens of Bohemia at their coronation.

Start at Obecní Dům (➤ 61) and head down Celetná to Staroměstské náměstí.

The leading burghers and dignitaries of the town rode out to welcome their new monarch at the Powder Gate (➤ 66), before accompanying him past the cheering crowds on Celetná (➤ 34) to Old Town Square (➤ 68). Here the procession halted to hear professions of loyalty from the rector of the University and the mayor and council in the Town Hall (➤ 22).

Cross the square to Malé náměstí and on to Karlova. At the end of Karlova, cross Křižovnická to Křížovnické náměstí (➤ 50) and the Charles Bridge (➤ 40).

Today Karlova is a quaint, twisting street, lined with galleries and souvenir shops, overshadowed by the fortress-like walls of the former Jesuit stronghold, the Klementinum (➤ 44). As the procession passed the Church of St Francis the King was greeted by the Order of the Knights of the Cross with the Red Star (➤ 50).

Cross the River
Vltava to Mostecká and follow Malostranské náměstí round onto Nerudova (➤ 60). Climb the hill to the Castle.

At the Lesser Quarter Bridge Tower, the mayor handed over the keys to the city and the King then continued through Malostranské náměstí (➤ 53) to the tumultuous sound of bells from St Nicholas's Church (➤ 48). The processional route ends at the Matthias Gate, the ceremonial entrance to Prague Castle.

Distance
2½ km

Time
1½ hrs without stops

Start point
Obecní Dům
✉ Náměstí Republiky
✚ 31C2

End point
Pražský hrad
✚ 30B3

Lunch
Dům U Červeného lva (££)
✉ Nerudova 41
☎ 537 239

Marionettes are among the more colourful souvenirs on sale in Staroměstské náměstí (Old Town Square)

49

30B3
Královsky letohrádek, Hradčany
Castle information: 2437 3368
Gardens summer only, Tue–Sun 10–6. Belvedere and Ball Game Hall open for exhibitions
Restaurant (£££)
22 & Few
Free
Pražský hrad (➤ 20–1)

Staroměstská

Dramatic sunrise over Křižovnické náměstí

31C2
Křižovnické náměstí, Praha 1
Exhibition: Apr–Oct Tue–Sun 10–7, Nov–Mar Tue–Sun 10–5
Staroměstská
17, 18 Cheap
Karlův most (➤ 40), Klementinum (➤ 44)

KRÁLOVSKÁ ZAHRADA (ROYAL GARDENS) ✪✪

These delightful gardens were laid out in 1534 in the style of the Italian Renaissance. Four years later, work began on the Belvedere, the handsome summer house presented by Ferdinand I to his wife, Anna Jagiello. A magnificent arcaded building with a copper roof resembling an upturned ship's hull, it was completed in 1564 by Paolo Della Stella, who also designed the mythological reliefs. The palace is now used for exhibitions. The sgraffitoed Ball Game Hall at the eastern end of the gardens is the work of the Czech architect, Bonifaz Wohlmut, and was given its name by courtiers who played a form of tennis here. Tulips grow in the gardens every spring – another reminder of Ferdinand I, who introduced the flower to Europe from Turkey in the 16th century. Near the entrance is the Lion's Court, once a menagerie exhibiting bears, panthers, tigers and other wild beasts.

KŘIŽOVNICKÉ NÁMĚSTÍ (KNIGHTS OF THE CROSS SQUARE) ✪✪

Dominating the eastern side of this square, which is named after the 13th-century guardians of the Judith Bridge, is the façade of the Klementinum and the Jesuit Church of St Saviour (➤ 44). The knights' own Church of St Francis, a baroque building which dates from 1679–88, is across the square. An exhibition at the side of the church includes a visit to the medieval crypt, which is decorated with garishly painted baroque stalactites. The

treasury contains a collection of jewelled monstrances, chalices, reliquaries and other religious objects which belonged to the Order, some dating back to the 16th century. Perhaps of greatest interest is a surviving span of the 12th-century Judith Bridge, complete with water stairs.

In front of the church, near today's Charles Bridge, is an imposing statue of Charles IV, designed in 1848 by Jan Bendl.

LAPIDÁRIUM ✪✪✪

Located in an art nouveau pavilion in the Exhibition Ground, this is a fascinating review of Czech sculpture from the 11th to the 19th century, with explanatory leaflets in English and other languages. One of the earliest exhibits is a beautifully ornamented column from the crypt of the 11th-century Basilica of St Vitus; other displays include the Krocín fountain, a remarkable Renaissance monument which used to stand on Old Town Square, and the 9m-high Bear Gate, also known as the Slavata Portal, which once adorned a beautiful baroque garden in the Smíchov district. Ferdinand Brokoff's statues of St Ignatius and St Francis Xavier, now adorning the Charles Bridge, are copies. The originals exhibited here were torn down in the floods of 1890.

+ 31D3
✉ Holešovice, Výstaviště 422, Praha 7
☎ 373 198
🕐 Tue–Fri 12–6, Sat–Sun 10–12:30, 1–6
🍴 Cafés (£)
Ⓠ Nádraží Holešovice
🚌 5, 12, 17
🚻 Few 👍 Moderate
↔ Veletržní Palác (➤ 26)

'Give peace a chance' is the sentiment expressed on Lennonova Zed'

LENNONOVA ZED' (LENNON WALL) ✪

Hidden among the embassies and palaces of the Malá Strana, this stretch of wall became a thorn in the side of the Communist authorities following John Lennon's death in 1980, when it was painted with democratic and pacifist graffiti. A game of cat-and-mouse ensued between police and artists as the wall was continually whitewashed and repainted. After the Velvet Revolution it was allowed to remain, at the request of the French ambassador.

+ 30B2
✉ Velkopřevorské náměstí
🚌 12, 27, 57
🚻 Good
👍 None
↔ Karlův most (➤ 40), Maltézské náměstí (➤ 54)

LORETA (➤ 19 TOP TEN)

MAISELOVA SYNAGÓGA (MAISEL SYNAGOGUE) ✪✪

Originally a Renaissance temple, built in 1591 for Mayor Mordechai Maisel (► 17), financier to Emperor Rudolph II, the synagogue has a beautifully restored interior, which preserves some of the 16th-century stone carving.

The building is now used to house an exhibition of sacred religious objects, which include items associated with the focus of Jewish worship – the Torah. This consists of the five books of Moses, handwritten on rolls of parchment by scribes. By tradition the rollers would be elaborately decorated with filials, shields and crowns, superbly wrought in silver or brass and often gilded or encrusted with jewels. Examples of the richly embroidered mantles in which the Torah was wrapped are also on display in the synagogue, along with other items such as spice boxes, silver goblets, paintings and engravings. But the most unusual exhibit is an enormous glass beaker, made in 1783–4 for the Prague Burial Society and painted with a procession of men and women dressed in funereal black.

<table>
<tr><td>✚</td><td>31C2</td></tr>
<tr><td>✉</td><td>Maiselova 10, Praha 1</td></tr>
<tr><td>☎</td><td>2481 0099</td></tr>
<tr><td>🕐</td><td>Sun–Fri 9–4:30. Closed Jewish hols</td></tr>
<tr><td>🍴</td><td>Restaurant (££) near by</td></tr>
<tr><td>Ⓜ</td><td>Staroměstská</td></tr>
<tr><td>🚊</td><td>Tram 17, 18, bus 135, 207</td></tr>
<tr><td>♿</td><td>Few</td></tr>
<tr><td>💰</td><td>Moderate</td></tr>
<tr><td>↔</td><td>Pinkasova synagóga (► 65)</td></tr>
</table>

MALOSTRANSKÉ NÁMĚSTÍ (LESSER TOWN SQUARE) ✪

The former market square of the Lesser Town dates from 1257. Looming over the charming ensemble of baroque buildings is St Nicholas's Church and former Jesuit College (► 16). Many of the arcaded houses have now been converted into cafés and restaurants, making the square an ideal place to linger.

The centrepiece of the square is the attractive Renaissance Town Hall (1617–22) on the eastern side of the square. Next door is the house At the Flavins, with a colourful fresco of the Annunciation.

<table>
<tr><td>✚</td><td>30B2</td></tr>
<tr><td>✉</td><td>Malostranské náměstí</td></tr>
<tr><td>🍴</td><td>Cafés £, restaurants ££–£££</td></tr>
<tr><td>Ⓜ</td><td>Malostranská</td></tr>
<tr><td>🚊</td><td>12, 22</td></tr>
<tr><td>♿</td><td>Few</td></tr>
<tr><td>↔</td><td>Chrám Svahého Mikuláše (► 16), Karlův most (► 41), Valdštejnský palác (► 71)</td></tr>
</table>

Did you know ?

A bust on the façade of the Kaiserstein Palace (No 23) honours the famous Czech soprano Ema Destinnová, who worked with the likes of Enrico Caruso, Giacomo Puccini and Richard Strauss in the early 20th century. The house's musical connections go back much further, to the occasion when Mozart heard a performance of Rosetti's Requiem here, led by another famous soprano, Josefína Dušková.

Opposite page: rooftop view over the crooked backstreets of Prague

53

➕ 30B2
✉ Maltézské náměstí
🍴 Restaurants (£££)
🚋 12, 27, 57
♿ Good
↔ Kostel Panny Marie
 Vítězné (➤ 46),
 Lennonova Zeď' (➤ 51)

Maltézské náměstí: the square has long been associated with the Knights of Malta

➕ 30B2
✉ Novotného lávka 1, Praha 1
☎ 726 5371
Ⓜ Staroměstská
🚋 17, 18
♿ None
🍴 Moderate
↔ Betlémská kaple (➤ 32),
 Karlův most (➤ 40),
 Křižovnické náměstí
 (➤ 50)

MALTÉZSKÉ NÁMĚSTÍ ✪
(MALTESE SQUARE)

This neighbourhood has been associated with the Order of the Knights of Malta since 1169. At the corner of Lázeňská is the former convent of the Order – Maltese crosses can still be seen on the main door and under the roof. Two impressive Gothic towers stand guard over the entrance to the Church of Our Lady Below the Chain, where a painting by Karel Škréta, decorating the main altar, depicts the victory of the Maltese Knights over the Turks at Lepanto in 1571. At the southern end of the square are two grand palaces: the brilliant pink-and-white Palais Turba, now the Japanese Embassy, and the ornate Nostitz Palace (open for chamber music concerts), which belongs to the Dutch Embassy.

MUZEUM BEDŘICHA SMETANY ✪
(SMETANA MUSEUM)

The life and work of the 'father of Czech Music', Bedřich Smetana (1824–84), are traced here through letters, documents, scores and musical instruments. Smetana studied piano and composition in Prague, where he heard Liszt and, later, Berlioz perform. A fervent patriot, whose music helped inspire the Czech national revival of the 19th century, he is best known abroad for his emotionally charged symphonic poem, *Ma vlast* (My homeland) – the famous second movement evokes the swirling currents of the Vltava. He also composed some fine chamber music, as well as numerous operas for the National Theatre, including *The Bartered Bride* and *The Kiss*. Smetana's later life was clouded by personal tragedy: in 1874 he went profoundly deaf after suffering from tinitis and later lost his reason, dying in an asylum.

MUZEUM ČESKÉHO SKLA (MUSEUM OF CZECH GLASS) ✪✪✪

Located in one of the historic houses on Old Town Square, this fascinating museum has two sections. Upstairs is a glittering exhibition on the history of Czech glass-making from the 14th to the 20th centuries. The displays range from beaded medieval flute glasses to gilt-etched drinking sets, made in Karlovy Vary in the 1920s by Ludwig Moser and sons. There are some exquisite examples of the baroque Bohemian glassware which drove the Venetians from the market in the 18th century, embossed Biedermeier vases with delicate painted decoration and ornamental glass of the art nouveau period. Downstairs, in the furnace, visitors are given a demonstration of the various glass-blowing techniques. The items produced here are on sale in the museum shop.

🞧 31C2
✉ Staroměstské náměstí 26, Praha 1
☎ 2422 9755
🕐 Daily 10–9
🍴 Cafés (££), restaurants (£££) near by
Ⓜ Staroměstská
♿ None 🞔 Cheap
🚋 Staroměstské náměstí (➤ 68)

MUZEUM HLAVNÍHO MĚSTO PRAHY (CITY OF PRAGUE MUSEUM) ✪✪

This interesting museum charts the history of Prague, and includes exhibits which range from the earliest times to the 20th century. Among the various household items on display are slippers, combs and a 14th-century wash-tub, as well as pottery and coins. The medieval craft guilds are represented in displays of tools, signs and seals, and by some fine examples of their workmanship, including a mural painting of 1406, originally executed for the House at the Golden Angel in Old Town Square. Weapons, model soldiers and cannons and the lock of the original Bethlehem Chapel door (➤ 32) are used to illustrate the Hussite period and there is an impressive collection of statuary, notably a wooden *pietà* from the Týn Church (➤ 46) and a stone Madonna which used to decorate the Oriel Chapel in the Old Town Hall (➤ 22). Another attraction is Antonín Langweil's ambitious model of 19th-century Prague, which can be illuminated to show different areas of the city.

🞧 31D2
✉ Na poříčí 52, Praha 1
☎ 2422 3696
🕐 Tue–Sun 9–6
🍴 None 🚇 Florenc
🚋 8, 24
♿ None 🞔 Cheap

Above: *An exquisite example of Bohemian glassware*

Above left: *glass-blowing demonstrations are an attraction in the newly opened Muzeum Českého Skla*

19th-century stained-glass panels illuminate the main staircase in the Muzeum Uměleckoprůmyslové

31C2

✉ Kaunický palác, Panská 7, Praha 1

☎ 628 4162

⏰ Daily 10–6

Ⓜ Můstek

Moderate

↔ Obecní Dům (► 61), Václavské náměstí (► 25)

31C3

✉ 17 listopadu 2, Praha 1

☎ 2481 1666

⏰ Tue–Sun 10–6

Ⓜ Staroměstská

🚌 17, 18, 51, 54

♿ None

Cheap

↔ Náměstí Jana Palacha (► 58), Rudolfinum (► 66)

MUZEUM ALFONSE MUCHY (MUCHA MUSEUM) ✪✪

This new museum allows you an opportunity to discover the work of one of the great masters of Art Nouveau, Alphonse Mucha (1860–1939). Mucha began his career in 1887, shortly after studying at the Academy of Arts in Munich, when he found work as a set painter and decorator in Vienna and Paris. His most famous early illustrations were the posters designed for the French actress Sarah Bernhardt. He settled in Prague in 1910, having spent several years teaching. Other examples of his work can be seen in Obecní Dům, the National Gallery and the Art and Industry Museum. The collection is a representative cross-section of works from the Mucha Foundation: paintings, drawings, lithographs, pastels, sculptures, photographs and personal memorabilia. The museum shop sells a range of souvenirs with eye-catching Mucha motifs.

MUZEUM UMĚLECKOPRŮMYSLOVÉ ✪✪
(MUSEUM OF DECORATIVE ARTS)

Once housed in the Rudolfinum, the museum moved to Josef Schulz's neo-Renaissance building in 1901, and boasts a rich collection of Czech and European applied arts. For the time being, only a fraction is on display in the three large halls, but there is plenty to enjoy. The collection of Bohemian glass dates back to the Renaissance and is outstanding, but don't overlook the Venetian and medieval exhibits. There are selections of Meissen and Sèvres porcelain, exquisite majolica tableware from Urbino and Delft and beautifully inlaid cabinets, bureaux and escritoires, from baroque to Biedermeier. The museum shop sells a wide range of art publications and catalogues, as well replicas and souvenirs.

A Walk Around the Castle Grounds

This walk explores the hinterland of Prague Castle, taking in Petřín Hill with its superb views across the city.

Begin at Hradčanské náměstí and head away from the castle.

In the middle of Hradčany Square (➤ 40) is a baroque Plague Column of 1726 and, near by, a wrought-iron street lamp – a relic from the days of gas lighting.

Walk along Loretánská. Turn right at the end to the shrine of the Loreta (➤ 19).

The carillon in the tower first rang out on 15 August 1695 (the Feast of the Assumption of the Virgin). If you happen to be here on the hour, you will hear the 27 bells play a popular hymn tune, *We Greet Thee a Thousand Times.*

Walk back to Loretánská as far as the junction with Pohořelec. Turn right into Pohořelec, past Úzov, then left into the Strahov Monastery (➤ 24).

On your left is the 17th-century Church of St Roch, patron saint of plague victims. Ahead is the Abbey Church of the Annunciation.

Enter the monastery courtyard through the medieval gateway to the left of the church and leave by the arch at the eastern end. Take the downhill path through the Strahov gardens (once the monastic orchards), then climb the steps to your right to the summit of Petřín Hill (➤ 64). Continue the descent by funicular railway to Újezd.

The funicular railway was constructed for the Jubilee Exhibition of 1891 and runs daily 9:15–8:45.

Ornate street lamps are a common sight in Hradčany

Distance
2km

Time
2½ hrs without stops

Start point
Hradčany náměstí
 40B1

End point
Újezd/ Karmelitská
🞖 30B2

Lunch
Nebozízek Restaurant (££)
✉ Petřín Hill
☎ 537 905 (book in advance)

NÁMĚSTÍ JANA PALACHA (JAN PALACH SQUARE)

🚩 31C3
✉ Náměstí Jana Palacha, Praha 1
🍴 Café (£) near by
Ⓜ Staroměstská
🚌 17, 18, 51, 54
♿ None
💷 Free
↔ Muzeum Uměleckprůmyslové (➤ 56), Rudolfinium (➤ 66)

Memorial to the Czech martyr of the Soviet occupation Jan Palach outside the philosophy building of the university where he studied

'Red Army Square' was renamed after the Velvet Revolution to commemorate Jan Palach, the 21-year-old philosophy student who burnt himself to death in January 1969 as a protest against the Soviet occupation of Czechoslovakia. The authorities were unmoved but more than 800,000 people joined the funeral procession to Olšanské cemetery, where his remains were laid to rest. On the east side of the square is the philosophy building of the university, where Palach attended lectures: on the lower left-hand corner of the façade is a small bronze death mask by Olbran Zoubek.

NA PŘÍKOPĚ (ON THE MOAT)

🚩 31C2
✉ Na příkopě, Praha 1
🍴 Cafés (£), restaurants (££)
Ⓜ Můstek/Náměstí Republiky
♿ Few
💷 Free
↔ Václavské náměstí (➤ 25), Prašná brána (➤ 66)

This busy, pedestrianised street takes its name from the moat which once formed a boundary between the Old and New Towns. Today it is one of Prague's major shopping thoroughfares, with some compelling architecture from the late 19th century, when a number of major banking houses established their offices here. Particularly impressive is No 18–20. Actually two buildings connected by a bridge, it was designed by Osvald Polívka and completed in 1896. The colourful mosaics in the lunettes are from cartoons by the Czech artist, Mikoláš Aleš.

NÁRODNÍ DIVADLO (NATIONAL THEATRE) ⭐⭐

Partly funded by public donations, the founding of a National Theatre in this striking building overlooking the River Vltava represented the re-emergence of Czech nationalism in the mid-19th century. The foundation stone was laid in 1848 to the accompaniment of folk dancing and celebrations, and when the almost completed theatre was destroyed by fire in 1881, the Czechs immediately began raising more money and finished a second National Theatre in just two years. The design by Josef Schulz closely followed Josef Zítek's original.

The decoration was entrusted to a group of artists who became known as 'the generation of the National Theatre'. The loggia facing Národní has five arcades decorated with lunette paintings by Josef Tulka, while the attic contains statues by Bohuslav Schnirch, Antonín Wagner and Josef Myslbek. The interior is even more resplendent: in the portrait gallery, Myslbek sculpted bronze busts of Smetana and other contributors to Czech opera and drama, and Mikoláš Aleš, Adolf Liebscher and František Ženíšek filled the foyers with paintings. The stage curtain depicting the story of the National Theatre is by Vojtěch Hynais.

✚ 30B2
✉ Národní 2, Praha 1
☎ 2491 3437
🕐 For concerts
🍴 Café-bar (££)
Ⓜ Národní třída
🚋 6, 9, 17, 18, 22, 51
♿ Few
↔ Betlémská kaple (➤ 32)

The auditorium of the Národní divadlo with a ceiling by František Ženíšek

NÁRODNÍ MUZEUM (NATIONAL MUSEUM) ⭐

This stolid neo-Renaissance building, crowned with a gilded dome, dominates Wenceslas Square. Serving up large but unimaginative helpings of natural history, mineralogy, palaentology, zoology and anthropology, the museum is worth visiting for the richly decorated Ceremonial Hall and Pantheon. Statues of famous Czechs compete with historical wall paintings and allegories of Science, Art, Inspiration and Power, all commissioned from Bohemia's best 19th-century sculptors and painters.

✚ 31C1
✉ Václavské náměstí 68, Praha 1
☎ 2449 7111
🕐 May–Sep daily 10–6, Oct–Apr daily 9–5
🍴 Café (£)
Ⓜ Muzeum ♿ Few
⚫ Moderate
↔ Václavské náměstí (➤ 25)

NÁRODNÍ TECHNICKÉ MUZEUM (NATIONAL TECHNICAL MUSEUM) ✪✪

✚ 31C3
✉ Kostelní 42, Praha 7
☎ 2039 9111
🕐 Tue–Sun 9–5
Ⓜ Vltavská
🚌 1, 26
♿ Few
💷 Moderate
↔ Veletržní palác (➤ 26),
Lapidárium (➤ 51)

Pilot's-eye view of the Transport Hall of the Národní Technické Muzeum

The vast, glass-roofed central hall is the main attraction of this museum, with its exhibition on the history of transport, featuring more than 500 vehicles, machines and models. Suspended from the ceiling is the skeleton of an early powered glider dating from 1905 and J Kašpar's Bleriot-XI monoplane of 1910. A magnificent steam engine and tender, built in Prague for the Austrian State Railways in 1911, dwarfs everything else in the locomotives exhibition, and a wonderful collection of early automobiles starts with an 1893 Benz 'Viktoria'. The Czechs' own Skoda Works are represented by a wood-upholstered fire engine from 1928.

Among the 40,000 items displayed elsewhere in the museum are film cameras, clocks and watches, astrolabes, sextants, phonographs and much else besides. Visits to the simulated mining gallery are by guided tour only.

NERUDOVA ✪✪

✚ 30B3
✉ Nerudova, Praha 1
🍴 Cafés (£), restaurants (££–£££)
🚌 12, 27, 57
♿ None
💷 Free
↔ Pražský hrad (➤ 20–1),
Chrám Svatého Mikuláše
(➤ 16), Malostranské
náměstí (➤ 53)

The sign of the house At the Three Fiddles on Nerudova

This street honours Pavel Neruda (1834–91), whose short stories capture perfectly the small-town atmosphere of 19th-century Prague, and who was born at No 47. It's a steep climb to the top – Nerudova was originally called Spur Street after the brake which was applied to coaches on their descent. On your way you will see some wonderful 18th-century house signs (numbers were not introduced until the 1770s). Look out for The Red Eagle (No 6), The Three Fiddles (No 12), The Golden Cup (No 16),

The Golden Horseshoe (No 34), The Green Lobster (No 43), the Two Suns (No 47) and the White Swan (No 49). Two magnificent baroque mansions, the Thun Hohenstein

Palace (No 20) and the Morzín Palace (No 5) are now the Italian and Romanian embassies. Nerudova leads eventually to Prague Castle, a wonderful vantage point from which to view the city.

Homage to Prague by Karel Špillar, mosaic on the façade of Obecní dům

NOVÝ SVĚT (NEW WORLD) ✪

One of the prettiest corners of Hradčany, Nový Svět is a country lane of quaint cottages dating back to the 17th century. Look out for U Zletého noha (At the Golden Griffin, No 1), where the astronomers Tycho Brahe and Johannes Kepler once lived and U Zlaté hrušky (At the Golden Pear, No 3), now one of Prague's finest restaurants.

- 30A3
- Nový Svět
- Restaurant (£££)
- 22 Few
- None
- Loreta (► 19), Strahovský klášter (► 24)

OBECNÍ DŮM (MUNICIPAL HOUSE) ✪✪✪

One of Prague's most engaging art nouveau monuments, Obecní dům was conceived as a community centre with concert halls, assembly rooms, offices, cafés and restaurants. Antonín Balšánek and Osvald Polívka won a competition for the design and it was completed in 1911. Each of the rooms has its own character, but there is overall unity in the stained-glass windows, inlaid floors, wrought-iron work and walls of polished wood or marble. Scarcely a Czech artist of the period failed to contribute to the interiors. The Smetana Concert Hall was decorated by Karel Špillar and Ladislav Šaloun; Alfons Mucha was responsible for the Mayor's Salon. Just as remarkable is Špillar's large mosaic, *Homage to Prague*, on the façade.

- 31C2
- Náměstí Republiky 5, Praha 1
- 2200 2111
- Café (£), restaurant (££)
- Náměstí Republiky
- 5, 14, 26
- Good
- Moderate
- Celetná (► 34), Na Příkopě (► 58), Prašná brána (► 66)

In the Know

If you only have a short time to visit Prague, or would like to get a real flavour of the city, here are some ideas:

10
Ways To Be A Local

A good sense of humour and a sense of the ridiculous are typical Czech characteristics, so be ready to share a joke.
Sample the atmosphere in a traditional beer bar (*pivnice /hospoda*), like U Zlatého tygra.
Check out the form at the races (there are hurdle and steeplechases, also trotting races ✉ Velká Chuchle course, Radotínská 69, Praha 5 ☎ 543 091).
It's polite to share a table in a crowded restaurant and a good way to get to know Czechs.
Take a short cut through the passageways off Wenceslas Square (➤ 25).
Learn a few words of Czech. Although an increasing number of Praguers are coming to terms with English, they'll appreciate your efforts.
If you're invited into a Czech home, take some flowers for your hosts.
Don't talk about Communism or the Russians. Many Czechs prefer to forget the occupation. A safer topic of conversation is the much-loved First Republic (the inter-war years).
Take a fast-food lunch with the office workers in the Franciscan Gardens.
Go and watch Prague's leading soccer and ice hockey teams (both called Sparta Praha) at a home game. You can buy their colours from a shop in Betlemské náměstí.

10
Good Places To Have Lunch

Café Louvre
✉ Národní třida 20, Praha 1
☎ 2491 2230. Upstairs restaurant (non-smoking room) with views of the Art Nouveau architecture on Narodní.
Ethno Café Bar
✉ Husova 10 ☎ 232 7940. Ethnic bric-á-brac, including Guatemalan wood carvings, African cane fans and exotic fabric parrots, provides the décor in this pleasant café.

Le Bistro de Marlene
✉ Plavecká 4, Vyšehrad
☎ 291 077. Round off your tour of the ancient fortress with the best French meal in Prague. Open for lunch Mon–Fri 12–2, reservations advisable.
Nebozízek Restaurant
✉ Petřínské sady
☎ 537 905. The food isn't special but the views from the terrace (reached by funicular) are spectacular. Popular, so reserve a table.
Pizzeria Rugantino
✉ Dusní 4, Praha 1
☎ 231 8172. Old Town restaurant, serving salads, pies and pizzas cooked in a wood-fired oven.
Slavia Kavárna
✉ Smetanovo nábřeži /Národní, Praha 1
☎ 2422 0957. Captivating views of the river and Mala Strana make this old fashioned café-restaurant special.
Take a picnic in the small park on Divadelní (near the National Theatre), where there are panoramic views of Prague Castle.
U Kalicha ✉ Na Bojišti 12 ☎ 290 701. Immortalised by Jaroslav Hašek's novel, *The Good Soldier Schweik*, U Kalicha cashes in on the literary connection with mugs and other memorabilia.
U Pešků ✉ Náměsti Miruq 9. Although catering mainly for Czechs rather than tourists, this traditional restaurant welcomes visitors.

Knedlíky (dumplings) are a common side-dish in Czech restaurants

U Zlatého Stromu
✉ Karlova 6 ☎ 2422 1385. 'At the Golden Tree' is an old hotel with a warm atmosphere. Dishes include Prague toast, chicken salad and pizzas (illustrated menu).

10 Top Activities

Ballooning: the following clubs include insurance and a certificate of 'baptism by ballooning' as part of the deal, Sky Tours ✉ Jiří Pašek, Mikuláše z Husi 2, Praha 4 ☎ 439 9544; Adyton ✉ Bulharská 16, Praha 10 ☎ 748 136; Stifter Balloons ✉ Moskevská 61, Praha 10 ☎ 731 128.
Bowling: Interhotel Forum ✉ Kongresová 1, Praha 4 ☎ 6119 1326.
Canoeing: on the Berounka River – experienced canoers and beginners (Saturdays and Sundays), Central European Adventures ✉ Jáchymova 4, Praha 1 ☎ 232 8879.
Cycling: Central European Adventures ✉ Jáchymova 4, Praha 1 ☎ 232 8879 arranges bicycle tours to Karlštejn and the Koněprusy Caves, also day trips around

Prague. Closed Mondays.
Fitness Centres: Hotel Axa ✉ Na poříčí 40, Praha 1 ☎ 232 9359; Fitness Club ✉ InterContinental Hotel, Náměstí Curieovych 43/5, Praha 1 ☎ 2488 1525.
Golf: There is an 18-hole golf course at Golf Club Praha (behind Hotel Golf) ✉ Plzeňská, Praha 5 ☎ 544 586. For something less strenuous the Erpet Golf Centrum offers an 18-hole virtual reality golf course, as well as astro-turf putting greens and driving platforms ✉ Strakonická 510, Praha 5 ☎ 548 086.
Jogging: there are plenty of open spaces for running in Prague including Stromovka Park, the Vyšehrad ramparts, around Strahov, Kampa Island and Letna.
Sports Centres: swimming, sauna, massage, squash, tennis and bowling are all available at Sportcentrum Hotel, Čechie Praha ✉ U Sluncové 618, Praha 8 ☎ 6631 1554; Clubhotel Praha ✉ Průhonice 400 ☎ 6775 0019.
Swimming: there are indoor and outdoor pools at Podolí ✉ Podolská 74, Praha 4 ☎ 6121 4343 and Slavia. ✉ Vladivostovská 2, Praha 10 ☎ 735 552. There is also a beach at Džbán Reservoir ✉ Šárka Nature Reserve, Praha 6, with a special section for nude bathing.
Tennis: there are clay

courts at Štvanice Lawn Tennis Club ✉ Štvanice Island, Praha 7 ☎ 2481 0272; SK Slavia Praha ✉ Letenské Sady 32, Praha 7 ☎ 370 391.

5 Things To Do On The River

- Dine on a terrace at the Kampa Park Restaurant ✉ Na Kampě 8b ☎ 5731 3493, overlooking the Vltava.
- Take a pleasure cruise with buffet lunch and live music. EVD, departing from Čehův most ☎ 231 0208.
- Take a stroll around the islands: Kampa (Malá Strana), Veslarský ostrov (Podoli), Císařská Louka (Smíchov), Slovanský ostrov Žofin (Nové Město).
- Hire a rowing boat from Rent-A-Boat ✉ Slovanský ostrov (with lanterns at night) or ✉ Půjčovna Romana Holana (daytime only).
- Feed the waterbirds on the Čertovka river.

5 Views of Prague

- From 'the metronome' on Letna Gardens – there used to be a statue of Stalin here.
- Across the Malá Strana from the Observatory in Petřín Park.
- Along the Vltava River valley from the ramparts of Vyšehrad.
- Views of Prague Castle and Hradčany from the Charles Bridge Tower (Old Town).
- Across the Staré Město from the tower of the Town Hall.

View from Petřínské sady across the Malá Strana (Lesser Quarter) to Pražský hrad (Prague Castle)

🚩 31C3
✉ U Starého hřbitova, Praha 1 ☎ 2481 0099
🕐 Sun–Fri 9–4:30
Ⓜ Staroměstská
🚌 17, 18, 135, 207
♿ Moderate
↔ Klausová synagóga (➤ 44), Starý židovský hřbitov (➤ 69)

🚩 31C2
✉ Národní třída, Praha 1
🍴 Cafés (£), restaurants (££–£££) near by
Ⓜ Národní třída
🚌 6, 9, 18, 22, 51
♿ None
💵 Free
↔ Václavské náměstí (➤ 25), Národní divadlo (➤ 59)

🚩 30B2
✉ Petřínské Sady, Hradčany
🕐 Tower: Daily, Apr, May Oct 9–6, Jun–Sep 9:30–8, Nov–Mar weekends 9:30–5. Diorama: daily Apr–Aug 10–7, Sep, Oct 10–5, Nov–Mar weekends 10–5. Observatory: Apr–Aug Tue–Fri 2–11, Sat–Sun 10–12, 2–7, 9–11, Sep–Mar times vary
🍴 Restaurant (£££)
🚡 Funicular
🚌 6, 9, 12, 27, 57
↔ Strahovský klášter (➤ 24)

64

OBŘADNÍ SÍŇ (CEREMONIAL HALL)

Once used for Jewish burial rites, the Ceremonial Hall is now used to exhibit drawings by some of the 15,000 children who were confined at the Terezín concentration camp. There are also poignant poems, school exercises and records left by the adult prisoners, including some fine paintings, sketches, diaries, even music – all reminders that the human spirit cannot be extinguished, even in the face of the most barbaric cruelty.

PAMÁTNÍK 17 LISTOPADU 1989 ⭐

In an arcade between Wenceslas Square and the National Theatre is a small plaque commemorating the incident that sparked off the Velvet Revolution in 1989. On 17 November a large crowd, made up predominantly of students, headed towards Wenceslas Square from Vyšehrad, where they had been marking the 50th anniversary of the Nazi occupation. When they reached Národní they were confronted by riot police who charged, leaving hundreds severely beaten. Actors and theatre employees immediately called a strike, which led ultimately to the formation of Civic Forum.

PETŘÍNSKÉ SADY (PETŘÍN HILL)

Petřín Hill, where pagans once made sacrifices to their gods and medieval monarchs executed their enemies, is today a cool, restful haven with panoramic views of the city. Crowning the summit is the baroque Church of St Lawrence; the ceiling fresco here depicts the founding of an earlier church in 991 on the site of a pagan shrine. The 60m-high Observation Tower, modelled on the Eiffel Tower in Paris, was built for the Jubilee Exhibition of 1891, along with the Mirror Maze and a diorama depicting a battle between the Czechs and the Swedes for control of the Charles Bridge in 1648. Encircling the hill is the Hunger Wall, built in 1360 by Charles IV to provide employment in a time of famine. Lower down the hill, near the funicular stop, is the Observatory and Planetarium.

PINKASOVA SYNAGÓGA (PINKAS SYNAGOGUE) ★

First mentioned in 1492, the synagogue was founded by Rabbi Pinkas and enlarged by his great-nephew, Aaron Meshulam Horowitz, in 1535. A women's gallery and an impressive council hall were added in the early 17th century. The synagogue is now a memorial to the Holocaust, the walls painstakingly painted in red and black letters with the names and dates of the 77,297 Bohemian and Moravian Jews who perished in Nazi death camps during World War II. (The original paintings were erased by the Communists when they closed the building in 1968, ostensibly to prevent flood damage.) During recent excavations, a medieval ritual bath and the remains of several wells were discovered in the basement, evidence that there was probably a Jewish place of worship on this site long before the time of Rabbi Pinkas.

- ✠ 31C3
- ✉ Široká 3, Praha 1
- ☎ 2481 0099
- ⏰ Sun–Fri 9–4:30. Closed Jewish hols
- 🍴 Café (£), restaurant (££) near by
- Ⓜ Staroměstská
- 🚌 17, 18, 135, 207
- ♿ Few
- 💰 Moderate
- ↔ Maiselova synagóga (➤ 53), Starý židovský hřbitov (➤ 69)

Did you know ?

According to legend, Rabbi Löw (1512–1609) created a golem from clay, water, air and fire. It had superhuman powers which it used to protect Josefov residents from persecutors. The golem gripped the popular imagination and has been the subject of books, films and even an opera, composed by Hanus Bartoň for Opera Furore in 1992.

The Calvary Chapel near the Observation Tower on Petřínské sady

31C3
Nové mlyny 2, Praha 1
231 2006
Tue–Sun 9–4:30
Náměstí Republiky
5, 14, 26
None · Cheap

Traditional Post Office sign in the Poštovní muzeum

POŠTOVNÍ MUZEUM (POSTAL MUSEUM) ✪

A philatelist's delight but of wider appeal, too, this unusual museum boasts a colourful collection of postage stamps from Czechoslovakia, the Czech Republic and Europe. The backdrop is an exhibition on the history of communications in the region, using prints, old signs and other ephemera. There are also temporary exhibitions, for example on the postal service in the time of Rudolph II. The frescos in the showroom are by the 19th-century artist, Josef Navrátil.

31C2
Náměstí Republiky, Praha 1
Daily 10–5 (6 in the summer)
Náměstí Republiky
5, 14, 26
None
Moderate
Celetná (► 34), Na Příkopě (► 58), Obecní dům (► 61)

The Prašná brána is one of Prague's most familiar landmarks

PRAŠNÁ BRÁNA (POWDER GATE) ✪✪

Work began on this sturdy Gothic tower, originally the most important of 13 gateways into the Old Town, in 1475, but was halted eight years later when rioting forced the King to flee the city. It still lacked a roof when Josef Mocker was asked to complete it in the 1870s. The gate acquired its name in the 17th century, when it was used to store gunpowder. Before then its functions had been ceremonial: coronation processions began here before moving off towards St Vitus's Cathedral. The tower is a fine vantage point for Old Town views.

PRAŽSKÝ HRAD (► 20–1 TOP TEN)

31C3
Alsovo nábřeží 12, Praha 1
2489 3205
Gallery Tue–Sun 10–6
Staroměstská
17, 18, 51, 54
Gallery: cheap
Muzeum Uměleckprůmyslové (► 56), Náměstí Jana Palacha (► 58)

RUDOLFINUM ✪

One of Prague's leading cultural venues, the Rudolfinum is also a fine example of neo-Renaissance architecture. It was designed by Josef Zítek and Josef Schulz in 1876 and named in honour of the Austrian crown prince, Rudolph of Hapsburg. Concertgoers will come to know the Dvořák Hall, home of the Czech Philharmonic orchestra (chamber concerts and recitals are held in the 'small hall'). The Galerie Rudolfinum is used for contemporary art shows and other events.

A Walk Through the Lesser Quarter

From Malostranská metro station take Valdštejnská to Valdštejnské náměstí.

The square is named after the Imperial commander, Albrecht von Valdštejn, whose palace straddles the east side (➤ 71). Behind the Ledebour Palace (No 3) are two attractive terraced gardens (open to the public), hugging the slopes below Prague Castle.

Take Tomásská to Malostranské náměstí. Walk along the east side of the square to Karmelitská.

Before crossing to Malostranské náměstí, stop to admire Dientzenhoffer's baroque church, St Thomas's (➤ 48). The lower part of the square was once the site of a gallows and pillory. Now café tables spill out onto the pavement outside the Town Hall.

Leave the square by Karmelitská and continue past Tržiště to the Church of Our Lady Victorious (➤ 46) which contains the celebrated statue of Il Bambino di Praga.

On the corner of Tržiště you pass the Vrtba Palace, which has a delightful terraced garden, constructed around 1720.

Cross Karmelitská and turn left down Harantova. Walk through Maltézké náměstí (➤ 54) and turn right onto Velkopřevorské náměstí, which leads down to the river.

Beyond the Lennon Wall (➤ 51) and the approach to the Vltava is a little bridge crossing the Čertovka (Devil's Stream). On your left is the waterwheel of the Grand Prior's Mill, which, in common with much of the area, belonged to the Order of the Knights of Malta.

Turn right and follow the river to most Legii, where you can catch a tram back to the centre.

Journey into the past: the picturesque Čertovka (Devil's Stream) waterwheel in the Malá Strana (Lesser Quarter)

Distance
2km

Time
2hrs without stops

Start point
🇲 Malostranská
✚ 30B3

End point
Most Legii
✚ 30B2
🚊 6, 9, 22, 57, 58

Lunch
Malostranská beseda
✉ Malostranské náměstí 21
☎ 532 528

STAROMĚSTSKÁ RADNICE (► 22 TOP TEN)

STAROMĚSTSKÉ NÁMĚSTÍ ✪✪✪
(OLD TOWN SQUARE)

As early as the 12th century Old Town Square was a thriving market place. Merchants from all over Europe conducted their business here and in the Ungelt (► 71), a courtyard behind the Týn Church. The square was also a place of execution: among the victims were the Hussite rebel Jan Želivský and the 27 Protestant noblemen who died here following the Battle of the White Mountain in 1620 (they are commemorated by white crosses set in the pavement in front of Old Town Hall). Jan Hus, the father of Czech Protestantism, died in Constance, but his monument, a stark sculpture by Ladislav Šaloun (1915), stands in the centre of the square.

Today Old Town Square is primarily a place of entertainment where buskers and street traders vie with circus acts and side-shows, and the Astronomical Clock on the Old Town Hall (► 22) performs its mesmerising hourly routine. But the square's chief glory is its architecture: the Renaissance and baroque façades of the houses, painted in pastel shades, conceal Gothic substructures and Romanesque cellars; many are decorated with sculpted house signs and other emblems. The beautiful rococo embellishments on the Golz-Kinsky Palace, dating from 1765 (No 12 east side) are by Kilian Dientzenhofer. Franz Kafka went to school here in the 1890s. Directly in front of the Týn Church, the ribbed vaulting in the 14th-century Týn School arcade has survived.

Renaissance sgraffito covers the façade of the house At the Minute in Staroměstské náměstí

STARONOVÁ SYNAGÓGA (OLD-NEW SYNAGOGUE) ✪✪✪

Founded around 1270, the Old-New Synagogue is the oldest in northern Europe and is still open for worship. A typical Gothic building with a double nave, its most unusual feature is the five-ribbed vaulting of the main hall, unique in Bohemian architecture. Other details to look out for are the stepped brick gables on the exterior, the grape clusters and vine leaf motifs above the entrance portal and the medieval furnishings, including stone pews. There are 13th-century Gothic carvings in the tympanum above the Holy Ark, and the iron lattice enclosing the *almenor* or *bimah* (the tribune from where the Torah is read) dates from the late 15th century. Suspended between two of the pillars is a large red flag embroidered with the Star of David and the traditional Jewish cap. It was presented to the community in 1648 by the Emperor Ferdinand in appreciation of its contribution to the Thirty Years' War.

- 31C3
- ✉ Červená, Pařížská, Praha 1
- ☎ 2481 0099
- 🕐 Sun–Fri 9–4:30 and services. Closed Jewish hols
- 🍴 Restaurant (££) near by
- Ⓜ Staroměstská
- 🚌 17, 18, 135, 207
- ♿ None
- 💰 Moderate
- ↔ Josefov (► 17)

STARÝ ŽIDOVSKÝ HŘBITOV (OLD JEWISH CEMETERY) ✪✪✪

One of the oldest Jewish burial grounds in Europe, the Old Jewish cemetery was founded in the early 15th century: the earliest grave, belonging to Rabbi Avigdor Kara, dates from 1439. There are approximately 12,000 tombstones sprouting obliquely from the earth like so many broken and decaying teeth. Beneath them lie more than 100,000 bodies, buried layer upon layer in the confined space. The cemetery closed in 1787. This was the last resting place of many prominent members of the Jewish community, including Rabbi Jehuda Löw (1609), legendary inventor of the Golem (► 65), the mayor and philanthropist, Mordechai Maisel (1601) and the renowned scholar, Rabbi David Openheim (1736). The earliest headstones are of sandstone and have plain inscriptions, but from the 17th century they are decorated with carved marble reliefs indicating the trade or status of the deceased – for example, a pair of scissors for a tailor.

- 31C3
- ✉ U Starého hřbitova, Praha 1
- ☎ 2481 0099
- 🕐 Sun–Fri 9–4:30. Closed Jewish hols
- Ⓜ Staroměstská
- 🚌 17, 18, 135, 207
- ♿ None 💰 Moderate
- ↔ Klausenova synagóga (► 44), Obřadní síň (► 64), Pinkasova synagóga (► 65)

Splendid Gothic backdrop of the Staronová synagóga in Josefov

69

31C2

Ovocny trh 1, Praha 1

2421 5001

For concerts

Café (££)   Můstek

None   Free

Karolinum (➤ 41),
Na příkopě (➤ 58)

*The restored auditorium
of the celebrated
Stavovské divadlo*

STAVOVSKÉ DIVADLO (ESTATES THEATRE)

This famous theatre was built in 1781–3 for Count FA Nostitz-Rieneck, who wanted to raise the cultural profile of the city. Only four years later, on 29 October 1787, the count had his wish when Mozart's opera *Don Giovanni* received its world premiere here after being rejected by the more conservative Viennese theatre managers. 'The people of Prague understand me', the composer is reported to have said after conducting the performance from the piano. In 1984 Miloš Forman shot the relevant scenes of his Oscar-winning film *Amadeus* in the auditorium, drawing attention to the need for renovation. That work has now been completed.

Off map 31D3

U trojského zámku 4,
Praha 7

689 0761

Sat–Sun 10–5

112 from Nádraží
Holešovice

Few

Moderate

TROJSKÝ ZÁMEK (TROJA CHÂTEAU)

Count Wenceslas Šternberg cut a swathe through the royal hunting grounds in order to build his version of Versailles at Stromovka. Work began on the striking red-and-white château around 1679. The palace itself is modelled on an Italian villa, but after the death of the original architect, responsibility for the project passed into the hands of a Frenchman, Jean-Baptiste Mathey. To honour the architect's intentions, it is necessary to approach the château from the south, where the formal French garden, restored in the 1980s, leads to an elaborate staircase decorated with heroic statues representing the 'gigantomachia' – the epic struggle between the Gods of

Olympus and the Titans. The château apartments now house 19th-century Czech paintings. Most of the ceiling paintings are by an Italian artist, Francesco Marchetti, but for the Grand Hall, the count turned to the Flemish painter, Abraham Godyn. His frescos are Šternberg's effusive tribute to his Hapsburg masters, notably Leopold I, whose triumph over the Ottomans at the gates of Vienna is symbolised by a Turk tumbling from the painting.

The southern approach to Trojský zámek, built by the Šternbergs in the 17th century

UNGELT

In the Middle Ages this courtyard behind the Týn Church was a centre of commerce, where merchants paid *ungelt*, or customs duties. There was also a hostel for travellers here. The complex of 18 buildings dates from the 16th century onwards and has been restored as shops, hotels and offices. The Granovský House, built for a wealthy tax collector in 1560, is one of the most distinguished Renaissance buildings in Prague, with sgraffito depicting biblical and classical themes and a magnificent loggia.

➕ 31C2
✉ Týnský dvůr, Praha 1
🍴 Restaurant in Hotel Ungelt (£££)
Ⓜ Staroměstská
♿ Good
↔ Kostel Svatého Jakuba (➤ 47), Staroměstské náměstí (➤ 68)

VÁCLAVSKÉ NÁMĚSTÍ (➤ 25 TOP TEN)

VALDŠTEJNSKÝ PALÁC A SADY
(WALLENSTEIN PALACE AND GARDENS)

The Imperial General, Albrecht of Wallenstein (1583–1634), was a swashbuckling figure who amassed a tremendous fortune before succumbing to a blow from the assassin's axe. High-walled gardens were laid out in front of the palace by Niccolo Sebregondi between 1624 and 1630. The ceiling of the triple-arched *salla terrena*, designed in the Italian Renaissance style by Giovanni Pieronni, is decorated with scenes from the Trojan Wars. An avenue of bronze sculptures by Adam de Vries leads from the pavilion (these are copies: the originals were taken by the Swedes during the Thirty Years' War). At the far end of the garden is the Riding School, now an exhibition hall.

➕ 30B3
✉ Valdštejnské náměstí, Praha 1
☎ 5132 4545
🕐 May–Sep daily 9–7
Ⓜ Malostranská
🚌 12, 22
♿ Few
💷 Free
↔ Chrám Svatého Mikuláše (➤ 16), Malostranské náměstí (➤ 53)

VELETRŽNÍ PALÁC (➤ 26 TOP TEN)

VOJENSKÉ MUZEUM, SCHWARZENBERSKÝ PALÁC ✪✪ (MILITARY MUSEUM, SCHWARZENBERG PALACE)

A visit to the military museum is also an opportunity to see inside this remarkable Renaissance palace, built for the Lobkowicz family in 1545–63 by Agostino Galli, and acquired by the Schwarzenbergs in 1719. The façade is decorated with eye-catching pyramidal sgraffiti, and the ceilings on the second floor, painted with scenes from the Homeric legends, are remarkable.

The recently restored museum contains a colourful collection of arms, armour, uniforms and other militaria, and paintings on martial themes. For the enthusiast there is a shop selling tin soldiers, medals, cap badges etc.

Antiquated cannon line a corridor in the Vojenské muzeum in Schwarzenberský palác

VYŠEHRAD ✪✪

Rising from a rocky hill above the River Vltava, the twin spires of Vyšehrad church are one of Prague's best known landmarks (the name means 'castle on the heights'). The early history of this ancient settlement is almost insepa-rable from the myths and legends surrounding the first dynasty of Czech rulers, the Přemyslids, who established a fortress on the rocky outcrop in the middle of the 10th century. Prince Vratislav II (1061–92) chose this as his residence and built a walled palace, the Basilica of St Peter and St Paul and a chapter house. It was at this time that the foundations were laid of St Martin's Rotunda, one of the oldest Christian buildings in Bohemia. By the mid-12th century, Prague Castle began to take precedence, but Vyšehrad's value as a stronghold was recognised by Charles IV, who reinforced the walls and (to emphasise his links with the Přemyslids) made this the start of his coronation procession.

Near the remains of the Gothic 'Spička' Gate (nicknamed 'spikey' for its flamboyant decoration) is an information office and café. The elaborate Leopold Gate of

Opposite: former artisans' cottages in Zlatá ulička, by Pražský hrad (Prague Castle)

1670 leads into the main compound. Past St Martin's Rotunda is the Old Deanery, which stands on the site of a Romanesque basilica – the foundations are open to the public. Little remains of the early palaces, although from the terrace on the fortified walls there are views of 'Libuše's bath', actually a Gothic guard tower, as well as splendid vistas across the Vltava Valley. In the middle of the palace gardens is a medieval well – the statues by Josef Myslbek were removed from the Palacky Bridge after being damaged during a bombardment in 1945. The Church of St Peter and St Paul has been rebuilt many times, most recently in neo-Gothic style by Josef Mocker. In a side chapel is a medieval panel painting of the Virgin of the Rains, dating from 1350. Vyšehrad cemetery was founded in 1860 as a burial ground for Czech national heroes: the composers Antonín Dvořák and Bedřich Smetana, the artist Alfons Mucha and the writer Karel Čapek are all buried here.

The ceremonial Leopold Gate at Vyšehrad, commemorating the Austrian Emperor

ZLATÁ ULIČKA (GOLDEN LANE)

This row of colourful little cottages, built hard against the walls of Prague Castle, originally provided homes for the archers of the Castle Guard. During the 17th century the palace goldsmiths moved into the area, giving the street its present name. Golden Lane gradually fell into decline and was little better than a slum when Franz Kafka was living at No 22 during the winter of 1916–17. Today souvenir shops have taken over the repainted houses, attracting crowds of sightseers.

41F2
Zlatá Ulička , Pražský hrad
Tue–Sun 9–5
Cafés (£)
Malostranská
22 None
Pražský hrad (► 20–1), Klášter Svatého Jiří (► 43)

Excursions

There are any number of possible excursions from Prague, many within an hour or two's journey by train or car. The variety of scenery may come as a surprise, from the craggy uplands of Český Ráj and the Krkonože (Giant) Mountains to the woodland slopes of the Berounka Valley. Further south around Třeboň is a wetland area of lakes and carp-rearing ponds, an ideal habitat for water birds; and there are other surprises in store: a fairy-tale castle on an isolated hill top, a gloomy limestone cave with dripping stalactites, a charming Renaissance town hall at the centre of a busy market square. The elegant 19th-century resort of Karlovy Vary is famous for its hot mineral springs; Plzeň and České Budějovice are both centres of the brewing industry, and the vineyards of Mělník date back to the reign of Charles IV.

' It was the place where the spirit could soar up to any heights, but it was also the place where there was in the atmosphere a barely perceptible smell of decay...'

IVAN KLÍMA,
Love and Garbage (1986)

Left: *Karlštejn Castle was a medieval stronghold of the Bohemian Kings*

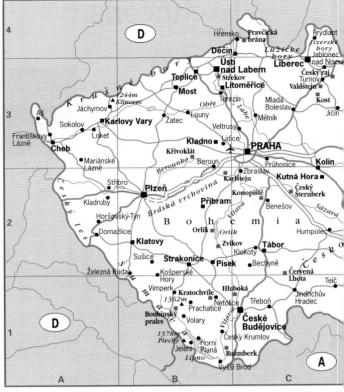

77D1

☎ Informační služba: 4221 1090

🕐 Town Hall: Apr–Sep daily 9–5. Castle: Jun–Sep Tue–Sun 9–6, Apr–May Tue–Sun 9–5, Mar, Oct 9–4

🍴 Cafés (£), restaurants (££)

🚇 Praha Hlavní Nádraží

♿ Few

💷 Cheap

❓ Sep: International Motorcycling Championship

BRNO

⭐⭐

The capital of Moravia and the second city of the Republic, Brno is famous for its Motorcycle Grand Prix and trade fairs, but it is also a lively cultural centre with several theatres (including the Reduta, where Mozart conducted his own compositions in 1767) and a number of interesting historical sights. Two Brno landmarks – the Špilberk fortress, which for centuries served as a Hapsburg prison and is now the city museum, and the Gothic Cathedral of St Peter and St Paul – stand on adjacent hills. Below the cathedral is the Old Town. It's worth climbing the tower of the Old City Hall for the views. Notice the middle turret of the hall's Gothic portal, which is askew: according to the local legend, it was left deliberately crooked by the builder as an act of revenge on the burghers for not paying his wages in full.

The fruit and vegetable market, one of the more colourful sights in Brno

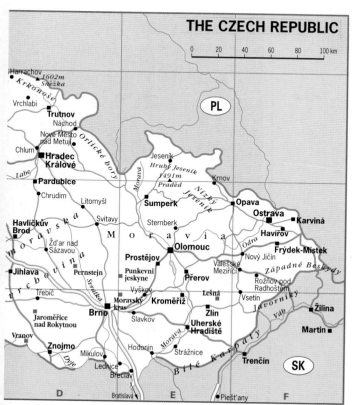

THE CZECH REPUBLIC

0   20   40   60   80   100 km

PL

SK

Right: *dramatic overview of Český Krumlov and the River Vltava from the castle*

Below: *detail from the Samson fountain in České Budějovice*

✚ 76C1
✉ Informační centrum: Goetz & Hanzlik, náměstí Přemysla Otakara II 2
☎ (38) 59 480. Brewery: 770 5111
🕐 Brewery: daily 9–3, for group tours
🍴 Cafés (£), restaurants (££)
🚉 Praha Hlavní Nádraží
♿ Few
🔁 Český Krumlov (➤ 79), Třeboň (➤ 90)
❓ Aug: International Agricultural Show

ČESKÉ BUDĚJOVICE ✪✪

This sedate old town was founded in 1265 by King Otokar II Přemysl as a base from which to attack his enemies, the unruly Vítkovec clan. During the Hussite Wars the mainly German population remained royalist and stoutly defended the Catholic cause. Commercially, the 16th century was a golden age as České Budějovice exploited its precious silver deposits, but the economic and social dislocation caused by the Thirty Years' War put paid to this prosperity and in 1641 the town was ravaged by a terrible fire which damaged or destroyed almost every building of importance. This led to large-scale reconstruction, which accounts for the mainly baroque appearance of today's town. The advent of the railways in the 19th century brought industry to the region and České Budějovice became the third largest city in the country after Prague and Plzeň. Today it is best known for its beer.

The town's main square, náměstí Přemysla Otakara II, is one of the largest in Europe: the Town Hall, a graceful building dating from 1727–30, the 13th-century Church of St Nicholas and the lofty Černá Věž (Black Tower) are the main attractions. It's a climb of 360 steps to the Tower's viewing gallery, but well worth it. A few minutes' walk away is the old meat market (Masné krámy), dating from 1564, now serving as a traditional beer hall. Visitors who develop a taste for Budvar may like to sign up for a tour of the famous brewery.

ČESKÝ KRUMLOV   ✪✪✪

Český Krumlov is simply ravishing. Surrounded by rolling countryside and the wooded Šumava Hills, the old town – a UNESCO World Heritage Site – nestles in a bend of the Vltava River. For more than 600 years its fortunes were inseparable from those of the aristocratic families residing in the castle: the lords of Krumlov, the Rožmberks, the Eggenbergs and finally the Schwarzenbergs, who were not dispossessed until after World War II. The castle is part medieval fortress, part château, magnificently set on a clifftop overlooking the town, and boasting a unique bridge resembling an aqueduct, a picture gallery and the oldest private theatre in Europe. Guided tours include a visit to the Hall of Masks, a ballroom painted in 1748 with *trompe-l'oeil* figures of guests attending a masquerade. The houses of the Latrán, the area around the castle, were originally occupied by servants and court scribes. Buildings here include a 14th-century Minorite Monastery and the Eggenberg Brewery, which still makes its deliveries by horse and cart. Below the castle steps is the medieval former hospice and Church of St Jošt, recently converted into private apartments.

The nucleus of the town is on the opposite bank of the Vltava. Prominent on Náměstí Svornosti (the main square) is the Town Hall, with attractive arcades and vaulting. Vilém of Rožmberk is buried in the Gothic Church of St Vitus, which dates from 1439. The Latin School, now a music school and the former Jesuit College, now the Hotel Růže, are also worth a look.

✚ 76B1
✉ Infocentrum: náměstí Svornosti 1
☎ (337) 711 183
⊙ Castle: Apr, Oct Tue–Sun 9–12, 1–3, May, Sep Tue–Sun 9–12, 1–4, Jun–Aug Tue–Sun 9–12, 1–5. Tower: Apr–Oct Tue–Sun 9–6
🍴 Cafés (£), restaurants (££)
🚉 Praha Hlavní Nádraží (via České Budějovice)
♿ None
⊘ Moderate
↔ České Budějovice (► 78), Třeboň (► 90)
❓ Mid–Jun: Five-Petal Rose Festival; Aug: International Music Festival

Above: *an extraordinary multi-tiered bridge crosses the ravine in Český Krumlov*

A Drive Around the Bohemian Uplands

Distance
131km

Time
8 hrs

Start/end point
Prague, Střížkov
➕ 76C3

Lunch
Radniční sklípek (£)
✉ Mírové náměstí 21
☎ (41) 66 626

Leave Prague, heading northwards on highway 608 to Bodanovice, then take highway 9 through Libeznice.

Crossing the River Labe, there are views of the vineyards which cluster around the delightful hilltop town of Mělník (➤ 86).

Continue on highway 9 to Dubá.

On your way you will pass through Liběchov, which has a château dating from 1730.

Turn left onto the 260 to Úštěk.

The ruins of Hrádek Castle will appear on your left as you approach Úštěk. This charming town posseses an attractive elongated square of Gothic and Renaissance houses, as well as the 'birds' cottages' built like nests on rocky promontories by Italian navvies who constructed the railway in the mid-19th century.

Leave Úštěk on highway 260, travelling northwards.

This scenic route crosses the forested Central Bohemian Heights (České středohoří), a designated area of natural beauty.

At Malé Březno turn left onto highway 261.

The road now tracks between the River Labe and its sandstone cliffs to the industrial town of Ústí nad Labem. On a promontory south of Ústí you will pass Střekov Castle, with its round Gothic tower. It is said to have been the inspiration for Richard Wagner's opera *Tannhäuser*.

Cultivating the hops in the beer-producing region of West Bohemia

ČESKÝ ŠTERNBERK ★★

Founded in 1242 on a sheer cliff above the Sázava River, the fortress home of the Šternberk family commands wonderful views of the valley. In 1660–70 the castle was remodelled in the baroque style by Italian craftsmen. The rococo Chapel of St Sebastian and the Yellow Room, with an elaborate stucco moulding by Carlo Bentano, are particularly beautiful. There is also a display of silver miniatures and a set of engravings on the staircase which depict scenes from the Thirty Years' War.

✚ 76C2
✉ Český Šternberk
☎ (0303) 55 101
🕐 Jul–Aug Tue–Sun 9–6, May, Jun, Sep Tue–Sun 9–5
🍴 Restaurant (££)
🚍 Bus from Roztyly metro
♿ None 🚶 Moderate
❓ Guided tour optional

HRADEC KRÁLOVÉ ★

Hradec Králové has been the regional capital of Eastern Bohemia since the 10th century. A Hussite stronghold in the 15th century, the town later featured in the Austro-Prussian war of 1866 as the site of the Battle of Königgrätz. At the heart of the old town is an attractive square (actually triangular in shape) known as Žižkovo náměstí after the Hussite warrior, Jan Žižka, who is buried here. Overlooking the square is the gauntly austere 14th-century Cathedral of the Holy Spirit. The free-standing belfry (71.5m high) is known, rather misleadingly, as the White Tower, and was added later. Just in front of the tower is a handsome Renaissance town hall. The Jesuit Church of the Assumption, on the southern side of the square, has an attractive 17th-century interior. Two leading art nouveau architects, Osvald Polívka and Jan Kot, worked in Hradec Králové. Polívka designed the Gallery of Modern Art, which has a superb collection of 20th-century Czech painting, while Kot was responsible for the Regional Museum of East Bohemia just outside the Old Town.

✚ 77D3
✉ Hradec Králové
☎ Information: (49) 34 021
🕐 Museum and Gallery: Tue–Sun 9–12, 1–5
🍴 Cafés (£), restaurants (££)
🚆 Praha hlavní Nádraží
♿ None
❓ Information centre: Gočárova třída 1225

The magnificent medieval fortress of Český Šternberk

- 76A3
- Kur-Info Vřídelní Kolonáda
- (17) 203 569
- Cafés (£), restaurants (££–£££)
- Coach from Praha Florenc
- Good
- May: opening of Spa Season; Jul: International Film Festival

KARLOVY VARY ⭐⭐

According to legend, Charles IV was out hunting one day when one of his hounds tumbled into a hot spring and the secret of Karlovy Vary was out. In 1522 Dr Payer of Loket set out the properties of the waters in a medical treatise and their fame began to spread. By the end of the 16th century there were more than 200 spa buildings – but the town's present appearance dates mainly from the 19th, when celebrities taking the waters included Beethoven, Chopin, Freud, Karl Marx and Goethe (who came 13 times).

There are 12 hot mineral springs in all, housed in five colonnades. The best known (and the hottest) is the Vřídlo, at 72°C, which spurts to a height of 10m. The wrought-iron Sadová and the neo-Renaissance Mlýnská colonnades preserve something of their 19th-century atmosphere.

Karlovy Vary comes alive in the summer, when there are concerts, theatrical events and festivals. The forested hillsides around the Teplá Valley are ideal for walks; the less energetic may prefer a gentle stroll along the promenade (Stará Louka).

Besides the curative waters, Karlovy Vary is famous for another, more potent liquid: a herb liquer called Becherovka after the doctor who invented the recipe while working at the spa in the early 1700s.

- 76B2
- Karlštejn
- (311) 681 617
- May, Jun, Sep daily 9–12, 12:30–6, Jul–Aug daily 9–12, 12:30–7, Oct–Apr daily 9–12, 1–4. Closed 1 Jan, 24–6 Dec
- Cafés (£), restaurants (££) near by
- Karlštejn from Praha-Smíchov
- None
- Expensive
- Křivoklát (▶ 83)
- Guided tour only

KARLŠTEJN ⭐

Perched on a cliff above the Berounka River, Karlštejn was founded by Charles IV in 1348 as a treasury for the imperial regalia and his collection of relics. In the 19th century the fortress was remodelled in neo-Gothic style by Joseph Mocker. Rooms open to the public include the wood-panelled Audience Hall, the Luxembourg Hall and the Church of Our Lady, which has a fine timber ceiling and fragments of 14th-century fresco painting. The magnificent Chapel of the Holy Cross in the Great Tower (closed for restoration) contains copies of 14th-century panels by Master Theodoric (the originals are in St George's Convent (▶ 43). The walls of the chapel are inlaid with over 2,000 semi-precious stones.

Taking the waters at Karlovy Vary. The distinctive spouted cup is de rigeur

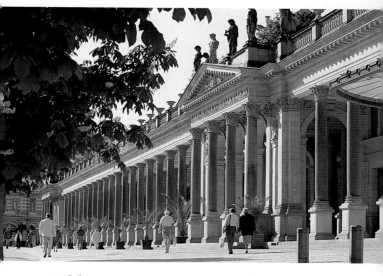

KONOPIŠTĚ ✪

In 1887 Konopište Castle was acquired by the heir to the Hapsburg throne, Franz Ferdinand, for his Czech wife Sophie Chotek. The Archduke's abiding passion was hunting – in a career spanning 40 years he bagged more than 300,000 animals. Some of the trophies line the walls of the Great Hall. Also worth seeing is Franz Ferdinand's impressive collection of medieval arms and armour and the landscaped garden with peacocks grazing on the lawn.

KŘIVOKLÁT ✪✪

This beautiful 13th-century castle, with its unusual 35m-high round tower, was once the royal hunting lodge of Charles IV. Inside is the vaulted King's Hall, a Gothic chapel with a fine carved altarpiece, a dungeon once used as a prison and now home to a grim assortment of torture instruments, and the Knights' Hall, with a collection of late Gothic paintings and sculptures.

> ### Did you know ?
>
> *Franz Ferdinand is a classic case of the hunter hunted. On 28 June 1914, while on a state visit to Sarajevo in Bosnia, the Archduke and his wife were gunned down by a Serb nationalist.*
> *Within six weeks Europe was at war.*

Konopiště
➕ 76C2
✉ Konopiště ☎ (301) 41 366
🕐 May–Aug Tue–Sun 9–12, 1–5. Closes at 4PM in Sep
🍴 Restaurant (£)
🚉 Benešov from Praha-Smíchov, then bus
💷 Expensive
↔ Český Šternberk (➤ 81)
❓ Guided tour only

Křivoklát
➕ 76B3
✉ Křivoklát
☎ (313) 558 120
🕐 Jun–Aug Tue–Sun 9–5, May, Sep Tue–Sun 9–4, Oct–Apr Tue–Sun 9–3. Closed 1 Jan, 24–6 Dec
🚉 Křivoklát from Praha-Smíchov, change at Beroun
♿ None
💷 Moderate
↔ Karlštejn (➤ 83)
❓ Guided tour only

Classical elegance – the Mlýnská kolonáda at Karlovy Vary

83

St Jacob's Church in Kutná Hora, one of the best preserved towns in the Czech Republic

76C2

Information: Palackeho náměstí 377

(327) 512 378

Italian Court: Nov–Mar daily 10–4, Apr, Oct daily 10–5, May–Sep 9–6. St Barbara's Cathedral: Nov–Mar Tue–Sun 9–12, 2–4, Apr, Oct Tue–Sun 9–12,1–4, May–Sep Tue–Sun 9–6 . Museum Hrádek: Apr, Oct Tue–Sun 9–5, May–Sep Tue–Sun 9–6. Ossuary: Nov–Mar daily 9–12, 1–4, Apr–Sep daily 8–12, 1–6

Cafés (£), restaurants (££–£££)

Praha Masarykovo to Sedlec, then bus

Coach from Praha Želivského metro station

Few

Jun: international guitar competition

KUTNÁ HORA ★★★

The name means 'mining mountain', and it was the discovery of large deposits of silver and copper ore in the 13th century which turned Kutná Hora overnight into one of the boom towns of Central Europe. A royal mint, founded at the beginning of the 14th century and known as the Italian Court, after Wenceslas II's Florentine advisors, produced its distinctive silver coin, *Pražské grosé,* until 1547. Visitors to the Court can see art nouveau frescos in the Wenceslas Chapel, as well as treasures from the Gothic Town Hall, which burned down in 1770, including a brightly painted wooden statue of Christ, *Ecce Homo* (1502). The Cathedral of St Barbara was endowed by the miners and dedicated to their patron saint. Petr Parléř's unusual design of three tent-roofed spires supported by a forest of flying buttresses was begun in 1388 but not completed until the end of the 15th century, when Matthias Rejsek and Benedikt Reid built the magnificent vaulted ceiling. Colourful frescos in the side chapels show the miners at work. Behind the town museum in Hrádek is a medieval mine where visitors are shown the *trejv,* a horse-drawn winch used for lifting the bags of ore.

North of Kutná Hora is Sedlec, where, in the 19th century, the Cistercian ossuary was turned into a macabre work of art by František Rint. There are bone monstrances, chandeliers and even a Schwarzenberg coat of arms.

A Drive Through the Berounka Valley

Take highway 4 south from Prague towards Stakonice. At Lehovice turn onto the 115 to Revnice (birthplace of tennis champion, Martina Navrátilová). Take the right fork onto the 116 to Karlštejn.

The main attraction here is the Gothic castle perched high above the church. You can also enjoy strolling through the village or sipping a glass of the local wine at one of the terrace bars by the river.

From Karlštejn church take the side road south (away from the castle) then the right fork at Korno, turning right again at Tobolka. Take the next left onto highway 114 to Koněprusy.

The village is famous for its 800m-long network of limestone caves, rich in stalagmites and stalactite formations. There is also an exhibition of finds, including human and animal bones and a clandestine illegal 15th-century mint. Open to the public Apr–Oct Tue–Sun.

Leaving Koněpruské caves, return along the 114, crossing the E50 to Beroun. From Beroun take highway 116 heading northwest along the Berounka Valley.

The river meanders through the Křivoklátsko, an area of dense forest and limestone buffs (now a UNESCO biosphere preservation area).

At Luby, turn left onto the 201, which winds round to the sleepy village of Křivoklát.

Křivoklát Castle (► 83) dates from the late 13th century and, although there have been some alterations to the structure over the years, the Gothic interiors are worth seeing.

Returning along the 201, turn left onto highway 236, leading out of the Křivolátsko at Lany. Turn onto highway 6 (E48) and head east for Prague.

Distance
130km

Time
6 hrs

Start point
Smíchov, Prague
✚ 76C3

End point
Břevnov, Prague
✚ 76C3

Lunch
Hotel Mýln
✉ 267 27 Karlštejn
☎ (311) 94 194

Tranquil scene on the banks of the Berounka River

85

76B3

10 Června 1942, Lidice

Daily 8–4

Bus (Kladno line) from Dejvická metro station

Few

Cheap

10 Jun: memorial day

Photo montage of the men from Lidice, massacred by the Nazis in 1942

LIDICE

In June 1942, following the assassination of the Nazi Governor of Bohemia and Moravia, Reinhard Heydrich, this small village was one of several arbitrarily singled out for reprisal. The men were herded into a farmhouse and shot, the women and children were transported to concentration camps and the entire village was razed to the ground. The site is now a shrine with a museum – a wooden cross and a memorial mark the actual place where the men were shot and buried.

77D2

Information: Smetanovo náměstí 72

(464) 612 161

Château: May–Aug Tue–Sun 8–12, 1–5, Sep 9–12, 1–4, Apr, Oct Sat–Sun 9–12, 1–4

Café (£), restaurant (££) in town

Few

Cheap

Jun–Jul: Smetana's Litomyšl (opera festival)

LITOMYŠL

This attractive town boasts one of the largest squares in the Czech Republic, with a Gothic Town Hall and an impressive array of Rennaisance and baroque houses. 'At the Knights', built in 1540, has a superb sculpted façade: attend an art exhibition here and take a look at the panelled Renaissance ceiling. The château was built in 1568–81 by the Italian architects, Giovanni Battista and Udalrico Aostalli. The exterior is decorated with stunning sgraffiti by Šimon Vlach and the private theatre is one of the oldest in Europe. Litomyšl is also famous as the birthplace of the composer Bedřich Smetana. His apartment in the château is now a museum and music festivals take place in his honour throughout the summer.

76C3

Turistické Informační st: Náměstí Mirů

Château: (206) 626 853

Château: May, Jun, Sep Tue–Sun 9–5, Jul–Aug Tue–Sun 9–6

Cafés (£), restaurants (££–£££)

Bus from Florenc coach station, Prague

None   Moderate

MĚLNÍK

Perched on a hilltop, with commanding views across the confluence of the Vltava and Labe (Elbe) rivers, is the château, Melnik's main tourist attraction. Founded in the 10th century, it originally belonged to the Bohemian royal family and was occupied by several queens, including the wives of John of Luxemburg and Charles IV, who is credited with introducing wine-making to the region. The castle passed into the hands of the Lobkowicz family early in the 17th century and they have owned it intermittently ever since. Mainly of baroque appearance, its northern wing has an impressive Renaissance arcade and loggia

Mélník Château and the Church of St Peter and Paul are reflected in the placid Labe River

with sgraffito decoration, dating from 1555. The rooms have been refurbished in a variety of styles; most interesting is the Large Bedroom, which contains an early 17th-century canopied bed with a painting of the Madonna at the head. Visitors are also shown trophies and mementos belonging to one of the château's more recent owners, Jiří Christian Lobkowicz, a talented racing driver who died tragically on a track in Berlin in 1932. There is a separate entrance charge for a tour of the remarkable 13th-century wine cellars, with tastings. Mělník's grapes are of the Traminer and Riesling varieties but the climate is not ideal for viniculture – the last good year was 1992.

Wine growing is celebrated in Mélník's annual festival

Tours are also available of the Church of St Peter and Paul, built in 1480–1520. Its extended nave is roofed with splendid network and star vaulting and decorated with Renaissance and baroque paintings, including work by Karel Skřeta. The 'pewter' font is actually made of wood. The main draw here is the crypt with its fascinating charnel house, stacked from floor to ceiling with orderly rows of heaped bones – some 15,000 of them at the last count. Some of the skulls are fractured or dented – the result not of careless handling but of bullet wounds sustained in the battles of the Thirty Years' War.

PLZEŇ

76B2

Information: náměstí Republiky 41

19 703 2750. Brewery: 722 4955. Museum: 224 105

Brewery: daily 8–3. Pivovarské Muzeum: Oct–May Tue–Sun 10–6

Cafés (£), restaurants (££)

Praha Hlavní Nádraží

Few Moderate

24 Feb: Plzeň Carnival

Beer has been brewed in Plzeň since 1295 and the Pilsner Urquell brewery is the main attraction in this largely industrial town. The guided tour of the cellars (there are 9km in all) includes a visit to the extravagantly decorated beer hall, definitely an experience not to be missed. Close by is a fascinating Museum of Brewing housed, appropriately enough, in a medieval malthouse. Plzeň's main square, Náměstí Republiky, has some fine Renaissance and baroque town houses and is dominated by the Gothic Cathedral of St Bartholomew, which boasts the tallest steeple in the country (102m).

TÁBOR

76C2

Infocentrum: Žižkovo náměstí 2

(361) 486 230

Town Hall Museum: May Tue–Sun 8:30–5, Jun–Sep daily 8:30–5, Oct–Apr Mon–Fri 8:30–5

Cafés (£), restaurants (££)

Praha hlavní Nádraží

None Cheap

České Budějovice(► 78), Třeboň (► 90)

Sep: Tabor Meetings, a festival of parades, music, jousting and events

Marvellously situated on a bluff commanding the Lužnice Valley, Tábor takes its name from the Biblical Mountain where Christ is said to have appeared transfigured to his disciples. After the death of Jan Hus, the Hussites transferred their allegiance to the one-eyed general, Jan Žižka, who continued the struggle against the Catholics. He encamped here in 1420 and held out successfuly for four years until his death in battle. The town's attractive main square, about 20 minutes' walk from the station, is called after him and there is a statue by Josef Strachovský.

The tower of the Church of the Transfiguration, which dates from the 16th century, offers the best views of the gabled Renaissance and classical houses and of the town itself, which is seen melting into the distance.

An exhibition in the neo-Gothic Town Hall presents an excellent account of the Hussite Movement. Don't miss the tour of the labyrinthine tunnels, 600m below ground. Dating from the 15th century, they were used variously as beer cellars, as a prison for unruly women and as an escape route in time of war. When you emerge, you'll find yourself near a café where you can sit and relax. The narrow twisting streets of the Old Town are a delight, although you may get lost from time to time. This is no accident – when the town was laid out Žižka's followers wanted to make life as confusing as possible for the enemy. A pleasant stroll along the banks of the Lužnice River leads to the Bechyň Gate and Kotnov Castle, with its distictive round tower. Inside are some fascinating displays on medieval life in the region, with costumes, archaeological finds, farming implements and weapons. The fabulous views from the tower are a bonus.

Only 2km away, across beautiful countryside, is the hamlet of Klokoty, with a baroque convent and church dating from the early 18th century. The wayside shrines along the footpath mark it out as a place of Catholic pilgrimage.

On the other side of town, between Žižkova and Tržní náměstí, is a Renaissance water tower decorated with vaulted gables and dating from 1497. The water was pumped to the town's seven fountains from the Jordan, the oldest dam in Europe, via a system of wooden pipes.

Above: *the 16th-century Church of the Transfiguration dominates the main square in Tábor*

Opposite: *equestrian statue of the Hussite leader Jan Žižka in Tábor's Town Hall Museum*

TEREZÍN

76B3
Information: náměstí Čs
Armady 84
(416) 92 369
Daily 9–6
Restaurant (£)
Coach from Praha
Florenc
None
Moderate

In 1942 the Nazis turned Terezín into a ghetto and transit camp for Jews. More than 150,000 people ended up in extermination camps, while a further 35,000 died of disease and starvation. At the same time the Germans used Terezín for their perverted propaganda purposes, persuading Red Cross visitors that this was a flourishing cultural and commercial centre. The exhibition in the main fortress gives an excellent if harrowing account of the realities of life in the camp, while, across the river, in the lesser fortress, visitors can tour the barracks, workshops, isolation cells, mortuaries, execution grounds and former mass graves.

TŘEBOŇ

76C1
Information: Masarykovo
náměstí 103
(333) 721 169
Château: May–Sep
Tue–Sun 9–noon, 1–5
Cafés (£), restaurants (££)
Praha hlavní Nádraží
Few
České Budějovice (▶ 78)

The ponds around Třeboň have been stocked with carp since the 14th century

The charming spa town of Třeboň is best known for the quality of its carp ponds, which date back to the 14th century – Carp Rožmberk is on the menu of many restaurants even today. Four surviving gates lead into the walled Old Town which has at its heart a beautiful, elongated square. Dating from 1566, the Town Hall is decorated with three coats of arms: those of the town and its wealthy patrons, the Rožmberks and the Schwarzenbergs. Opposite is the 16th-century White Horse Inn, which has an unusual turreted gable. Třeboň has its own brewery and horse-drawn drays deliver Regent beer to the local hotels and restaurants. The Augustinian monastery church of St Giles dates from 1367 and contains a number of Gothic features, including a statue of the Madonna. The attractive Renaissance château is open to the public and was built in 1562 by the Rožmberk family.

Where To...

Above: *Staroměstské náměstí café*
Right: *At the Two Cats bar*

Restaurants

Prices
Prices are approximate, based on a three-course meal for one without drinks and service:

£££ = over 1000Kč
££ = 500Kč–1000Kč
£ = under 500Kč

Ambiente (££)
A colourful Czech-owned restaurant which specialises in American cuisine. The servings of ribs, chicken wings, spinach baked potato and pesto pasta are invariably generous. Booking is advised.
Mánesova 59, Praha 2
627 5913 Jiřího z Poděbrad

Buffalo Bills (££)
A Tex-Mex eaterie offering the usual *fajitas*, *tacos*, *quesadillas* etc. Informal atmosphere with country music.
Vodičkova 9, Praha 1
2494 8624 Můstek
3, 9, 14, 24, 52, 53, 55, 56

Café Louvre (£)
Franz Kafka used to discuss philosophy here in the early 1900s. The upstairs restaurant is a friendly, no-frills eating house which keeps pool tables in the back room.
Národní třída 20, Praha 1
297 665 Národní třída
6, 9, 18, 22, 51

Caffè-Ristorante Italia (££)
Traditional Italian specialities are served in this bright, modern restaurant on one of the loveliest streets in Prague, not far away from the castle.
Nerudova 17 530 386
22

Cerberus (££)
Locals and ex-patriates rate this attractive, modern restaurant highly for its excellent Czech dishes, especially the game.
Soukenická 19, Praha 1
2481 4118 Náměstí Republiky

Chez Marcel (££)
A pleasant, modern restaurant serving simple but excellent French country fare, for example, quiches, grilled rabbit in mustard and French mussels.
Haštalská 12, Praha 1
231 5676 Náměstí Republiky 5, 14, 26

Čínské zátisí (£££)
Prague's ethnic restaurants are not always entirely reliable, but this Chinese establishment is a noteworthy exception to the rule. Particularly recommended are the soups and the beef dishes.
Batelovská 120/5, Praha 4
6121 8088 Budějovická

Circle Line Brasserie (££)
Formerly the Avalon Bar and Grill, Circle Line Brasserie offers two excellent value brunch menus. Specialising in French cuisine.
Malostranské náměstí 12, Praha 1 5753 0021/3 12, 22

David (£££)
Reservations are essential in this rather formal, attractively situated restaurant in the Malá Strana. Mainly meat dishes with a continental flavour.
Tržiště 21, Praha 1 5753 3109 12, 27, 57

Dolly Bell (££)
Although slightly off the beaten track, this welcoming Balkan restaurant is well worth seeking out. The southern European specialities include *burek* (meat and potato pastries), and moussaka and kebabs are the order of the day.
Neklanova 20, Praha 2
298 815 Vyšehrad

Don Giovanni (££)
A welcoming trattoria, only a stone's throw from the Vltava. The wild mushroom risotto is recommended. The owner prides himself on offering more than 30 varieties of home-made grappa.

✉ Karolíny světlé 34, Praha 1
☎ 2222 2060 🚊 17, 18, 51, 54

Dynamo (££)
A useful spot for lunch in a back street location not far from the National Theatre. The menu includes potato wedges, spicy chicken, peppered steak with corn on the cob and tagliatelle.

✉ Pštrossova 29, Praha 1
☎ 294 224

Fakhreldine (£££)
It's worth shelling out to eat in one of Prague's finest ethnic restaurants. The service is first class, and the freshly baked Arabic bread is a treat in itself.

✉ Klimentská, Praha 1
☎ 2223 2616 🚇 Florenc

Gargoyles (£££)
Run by an ambitious young American chef, this spacious modern restaurant, with live music at weekends, offers an eclectic and imaginative menu. Try the halibut with couscous and spinach salad or the grilled pork chop with roasted pear and potato fennel gratin.

✉ Opatovická 5, Praha 1
☎ 2491 6047

Hanavsky Pavilon (£££)
The location of this restaurant, in an iron constructed neo-Baroque pavilion in Letná Park, is a definite bonus. Diners are attracted by the expensive but delicious international and Czech dishes.

✉ Letenské sady, Praha 6
☎ 325 792 🚇 Malostranská
🚊 12

Il Ritrovo Spagheteria (££)
Particularly popular with the Italian business community of Prague, this is a reliable and friendly restaurant offering a wide range of antipasti.

✉ Lublaňska 11, Praha 2
☎ 296 529 🚇 IP Pavlova
🚊 6, 11

Jewel of India (£££)
This American-owned restaurant is a welcome addition to the international scene. The Mughal (north Indian) dishes include *murgh tikka masala* and *rogan josh*.

✉ Pařížská 20, Praha 1
☎ 2481 1010

Kampa Park (£££)
A wonderful location on Kampa Island, overlooking the Vltava. This restaurant (part of the Bacchus chain) offers a softly lit ambience and delightful specialities, including fresh lobster and game. Reservations essential for the terrace.

✉ Na Kampě 8b, Praha 1
☎ 5731 3493
🚇 Malostranská 🚊 Tram 22 to Malostranské náměstí

La Provence (£££)
Robert Chejn, the chef at this currently very popular (and therefore very busy) French restaurant, presents the usual Gallic specialities, from cassoulet to coq au vin. Attentive service but some of the waiters are over-anxious about tips.

✉ Štupartská 9, Praha 1
☎ 232 4801 🚇 Náměstí Republiky

The Nut Trick
When eating out in Prague expect to pay for everything – few restaurateurs are in the habit of offering a free aperitif or a liqueur. Even the nibbles carry a price tag, as you may discover to your cost when the bill arrives and you are charged more for the nuts than for the appetiser. The best advice is send them back before you order and always say no unless you are a personal friend of the manager!

Culinary Delights

Eating out has never been more enjoyable in a city which now boasts more than 150 cafés, restaurants and bars serving food. No longer do visitors have to queue outside for a table or suffer slow, surly service and meals high on quantity but low on everything else. Prague is also becoming more international in its culinary habits. Italian trattorias and pizzerias currently lead the field, but hot on the trail are the Americans, the French, the Japanese, the Yugoslavs and the Lebanese.

La Perle de Prague (£££)

Located in the arresting Tančici dům (one of the finer examples of modern architecture), this French restaurant has unbeatable views of the Vltava.

✉ Rašinovo nábřeží 80, Praha 2, by Jiráskův bridge ☎ 2198 4160 🚋 3, 17, 21

Le Bistro de Marlène (£££)

A little out of the way unless you happen to be visiting Vyšehrad, this excellent French restaurant is run by highly resourceful owner/chef Marlène Salomon.

✉ Plavecká 4, Praha 2 ☎ 291 077 🚋 7, 18, 24

Magdaleny Dobromily Rettigové (££)

Named after the Mrs Beaton of Czech cooking, this restaurant serves traditional dishes, washed down with dark beer.

✉ Truhlářská 4 ☎ 231 4483 🚇 Náměstí Republiky

Malostranská Beseda (££)

A pub and restaurant located in the former Malá Strana Town Hall. You can either confine yourself to a snack or indulge in the reasonably priced Czech and international menu.

✉ Malostranské náměstí 21, Praha 1 ☎ 535 528 🚇 Malostranská 🚋 12, 27, 57

Metamorphis (££–£££)

Beautifully situated in the restored Tyn courtyard, the restaurant is housed in an atmospheric 17th-century cellar. If you're overwhelmed by the Czech fare here, the café upstairs serves simple but tasty pasta and other Italian dishes.

✉ Týnský Dvůr ☎ 2482 7058

Miyabi (££)

Miyabi is owned by a Czech who lived in Japan for many years. The menu is a deliciously ingenious mixture of home-grown Czech ingredients cooked in a Japanese style.

✉ Navratilova 10, Praha 1 ☎ 295 376 🚇 Můstek 🚋 3, 9, 14, 24, 52, 53

Na rybárně (££)

One of Václav Havel's favourite eateries in the days before he became president, this homely fish restaurant offers tasty dishes such as 'sea devil' and grilled trout. Vegetarian dishes available on request.

✉ Gorazdova 17, Praha 2 ☎ 299 795 🚇 Karlovo náměstí 🚋 3, 4, 14, 16

Obecní dům (£–£££)

There are several dining spaces in this wonderful Art Nouveau monument. The most formal (and the most dazzling) is the so-called French restaurant (the cuisine is international). Downstairs there's the Plzenská Czech Restaurant, designed like a beer keller; while the café on the ground floor serves pancakes and other snacks (➤ 61).

✉ Náměstí Republiky 5, Praha 1 ☎ 2200 2777 🚇 Náměstí Republiky

Pálffy Palác (£££)

Dine out in the baroque surroundings of this sumptuous 17th-century palace beneath Prague Castle. The food, too, lives up to expectations. Reservations advisable.

✉ Valdštejnská 14, Praha 1 ☎ 5731 2243 🚇 Malostranská 🚋 22

Pizzeria Kmotra (££)

So popular that queues often stretch into the street, this excellent restaurant offers a wide range of pizza fillings.

✉ **Vjirchářích 12, Praha 1**
☎ **2491 5809** 🚇 **Národní třída**
🚊 **6, 9, 18, 22, 51**

Pizzeria Rugantino (££)

A good lunchtime stopover for visitors to Josefov: the pizzas here are satisfying.

✉ **Dušní 4, Praha 1** ☎ **231 8172** 🚊 **17**

Red Hot and Blues (££)

A lively Cajun /Tex-Mex restaurant which serves tasty shrimp gumbo, bean burritos and the usual range of burgers. Brunch served until 4PM, Sat and Sun.

✉ **Jakubská 12, Praha 1**
☎ **231 4639** 🚇 **Náměstí Republiky** 🚊 **5, 14, 26**

Restaurant U Cedru II (£££)

'At the Cedar' offers Lebanese and international cuisine, served amidst live music and belly dancing. Concentrate on the starters.

✉ **Na kocínce 3, Praha 6**
☎ **312 2974** 🚇 **Dejvická**

Reykjavik (££)

Fish soup and salmon are among the dishes on offer in this stylish restaurant. Efficient, friendly service.

✉ **Karlova 20, Praha 1**
☎ **2422 9251** 🚇 **Staroměstská**
🚊 **17, 18, 51, 54**

Sakura (£££)

Tempura, *sushi* and *sashimi* prepared from original ingredients imported directly from Tokyo by Japanese chef, Tsuda Hachiro.

✉ **Štefánikova 7, Praha 5**
☎ **542 348** 🚇 **Anděl**
🚊 **6, 9, 21**

Saté Grill (£)

A small, unpretentious Indonesian restaurant, which serves cheap, spicy chicken and meat dishes – handy for lunch after sightseeing in Hradčany.

✉ **Pohořelec 3, Praha 1**
☎ **532 113** 🚊 **22**

Taj Mahal (££)

The décor is nothing to write home about but the Indian food, mainly standards like chicken *tikka masala*, is surprisingly good.

✉ **Škretova 10, Praha 2**
☎ **2423 5671** 🚇 **Muzeum**
🚊 **11**

U Kalicha (£££)

Immortalised in Jaroslav Hašek's novel *The Good Soldier Schweik* (you can see the green-uniformed hero on the sign outside), this restaurant is specially popular with tourists and serves traditional Czech fare.

✉ **Na Bojišti 12-14, Praha 2**
☎ **290 701** 🚇 **IP Pavlova**
🚊 **4, 6, 15, 16, 22**

U Maltézských Rytířů (££)

An attractively sedate restaurant in the Malá Strana. Delicious Czech cuisine with the emphasis on game, although salmon and other fish are also on the menu. Book ahead for a table in the Gothic cellar.

✉ **Prokopská 10, Praha 1**
☎ **5753 3666** 🚊 **12, 27, 57**

U Mecenáše (£££)

Fresh game dishes are served in this luxurious establishment with vaulted ceilings and medieval beams.

✉ **Malostranské náměstí 10, Praha 1** ☎ **533 881**
🚇 **Malostranská** 🚊 **12, 27, 57**

Late Breakfast

One consequence of the post-1989 American invasion of Prague has been the increasing availability of Sunday brunch. Options range from the vegetarian menu at Radost FX (➤ 97) to the traditional ham and eggs at Molly Malone's. For a touch of spice try Red Hot and Blues (➤ 95), which serves up *huevos rancheros*, Mexican-style. Or, if the money is burning a hole in your wallet, there is always the buffet at V Zátiší (➤ 96), with its large selection of cold cuts, salads and omelettes made to order.

Dumplings

Bohemian dumplings (*knedlíky*) are made from bread, potato dough, soft curd or flour. Necessary accompaniments to meat dishes to soak up the grease and beer, they also come in more sophisticated guises, the best-known being fruit dumplings. The most mouth-watering versions are filled with plums, strawberries, sour cherries or apricots, with a topping of melted butter and icing sugar – not good for the waistline!

U Modré Růže (£££)

Such exotic dishes as turtle soup, ostrich and alligator are served in an elegant 15th-century wine cellar. There is an additional 50Kčs per person cover charge for the pianist.
✉ **Rytířská 16, Praha 1** ☎ **261 081** Ⓜ **Můstek**

U tří houslič (££)

'At the Three Fiddles' dates from the 16th century and was once owned by a violin maker. There are set menu options drawing from the à la carte list of fish and game specialities.
✉ **Nerudova 12, Praha 1** ☎ **535 0121** 🚊 **22**

U Vladaře (£££)

Attractively located in Maltese Square, this expensive but high quality restaurant specialises in old Prague favourites – such dishes as leg of boar in garlic and juniper berries, for instance, and roast goose with cabbage and three kinds of dumplings!
✉ **Maltézské náměstí 10, Praha 1** ☎ **538 128** 🚊 **12, 27, 57**

U Zlaté hrušky (£££)

'At the Golden Pear' enjoys a romantic location in a lane behind Prague Castle. Beautifully prepared international dishes with a French accent.
✉ **Nový Svět 3, Praha 1** ☎ **2051 4778** 🚊 **22**

Villa Voyta (£££)

Situated in a charming art nouveau villa, dating from 1912, this expensive restaurant is well worth the drive into the suburbs for its Bohemian-flavoured international cuisine. Particularly recommended are the grilled goats' cheese or cream of broccoli soup, followed by medallions of venison.
✉ **K Novému dvoru 124/54, Praha 4** ☎ **472 5111**

Vltava (£)

Set close to the River Vltava, this restaurant serves up enormous and delicious helpings of carp and trout with a creamy fish soup to start. Excellent value.
✉ **Rašínovo nábřeží, Praha 2 (near Palackého Bridge)** ☎ **294 964** Ⓜ **Karlovo náměstí** 🚊 **3, 7, 16, 17, 21**

V Zátiší (££)

One of relatively few restaurants to cater for vegetarians, V Zátiší attracts a loyal clientele, drawn to the food as well as to the intimate surroundings. Set menus are offered, as well as à la carte.
✉ **Liliová 1, Praha 1** ☎ **2222 1155** 🚊 **17, 18, 51, 54**

Zemský Dům (£££)

Nicely situated in the former Jesuit hostel near St Nicholas Church, this restaurant serves a range of attractively presented Czech and international dishes.
✉ **Malostranské náměstí 25, Praha 1** ☎ **530 214** Ⓜ **Malostranská** 🚊 **12, 27, 57**

Zlatá Ulička (££)

Nowhere near Golden Lane, despite the name, this friendly, unpretentious restaurant serves its customers generous helpings of traditional Yugoslav dishes.
✉ **Masná 9, Praha 1** ☎ **232 0884** Ⓜ **Náměstí Republiky**

Cafés

Bohemia Bagel (£)

A friendly self-service café where you can eat freshly-baked bagels until they come out of your ears. They also do regular sandwiches, quiches, brownies and cookies.

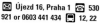 Újezd 16, Praha 1 ☎ 530 921 or 0603 441 434 🚊 12, 22

Café de Paris (££)

Admire the arresting Art Nouveau interior of this sedate hotel café. There is excellent jazz served up on Thursdays and Gateau Paříž every day.

✉ U Obecního domu 1, Praha 1 ☎ 2422 2151 🚇 Náměstí Republiky

Café Ledebour (££)

Although the food is not particularly remarkable, the most attractive thing about this café is the setting. It is housed in an old palace coaching house with a glorious painted baroque ceiling.

✉ Valdštejnské náměstí 3, Praha 1 🚇 Malostranská

Café Milena (£)

This is part of the Franz Kafka centre, which aims at promoting tolerance and understanding between different peoples. Attractively modern, the café is especially busy between 4 and 6PM, when a pianist plays for the guests.

✉ Staroměstské náměstí 22, Praha 1 ☎ 260 843 🚇 Staroměstská

Café Savoy (££)

An elegant café which enjoys a prime riverside locale.

✉ Vitězná 5, Praha 5 ☎ 539 796 🚊 6, 9, 22, 57

Country Life (£)

Central self-service vegetarian restaurant where all the dishes use only plant based ingredients.

✉ Melantrichova, Praha 1 ☎ 2421 3366 🚇 Můstek

Kavárna ve Šternberskén Palčí (£)

A haven for non-smokers, this newly opened café situated in the Šternberg Palace serves salads and snacks at very reasonable prices. Open only during gallery hours.

✉ Hradčanské náměstí 15, Praha 1 ☎ (gallery) 2451 0594 🚊 22

Radost FX Café (££)

A favourite with ex-patriates, the 'Fun' café is not really the place to come to meet local Czechs. The all-vegetarian menu is a definite draw for its relative novelty. Weekend brunch.

✉ Bělehradská 120, Praha 2 ☎ 2425 4776 🚊 6, 11

Restaurant Jarmark (£)

Amazingly cheap self-service restaurant in the Lucerna Passage. There are appetising salads, grills, stir-fries, pastries, fresh fruit and more. No one ever leaves hungry!

✉ Vodičkova, Praha 1 ☎ 2423 3733 🚊 3, 9, 14, 24

The Globe Bookstore and Coffeehouse (£)

This café offers an enjoyable mix of coffee, English conversation and tempting American-style desserts such as brownies and muffins.

✉ Pstrosova 6, Praha 1 ☎ 2491 6264 🚇 Národní třída 🚊 6, 9, 17, 21, 22, 23, 51, 54, 58

Time for Tea

Like Vienna, Prague is traditionally more associated with coffee houses than with tea rooms, but the latter are proving increasingly popular, especially with visitors. Two to try: Dobrá čajovna, ✉ Václavské náměstí 14, and U Zeleného čaje, ✉ Nerudova 19, which serves vegetarian pizzas, salads and tofu and sells teapots, mugs, honey, joss sticks and other accessories.

Restaurants Outside Prague

Spirit of the Times?
Following a court ruling in favour of the German firm of Underberg, Becherovka, the famous liqueur associated with Karlovy Vary since it was invented in 1807, will be produced in Germany as well as the Czech Republic. The dispute has cost the Karlovarská Becherovska distillery an estimated 40 per cent of the German export market and Underberg are expected to acquire a significant holding in the firm when it is privatised.

Brno

Zahradní Restaurace (££)
The 'Garden Restaurant' has long been celebrated for its Chinese cuisine, but the Moravian dishes, heavily laced with paprika, are also worth trying. Pleasant ambience and very reasonable prices.
✉ **Grandhotel Brno, Benešova 18–20** ☎ **(5) 4232 1287**

České Budějovice

Masné Krámy (£)
A menu of plain but substantial Czech fare served up in the historic surroundings of the old meat market.
✉ **Krajinská 13** ☎ **(38) 731 8615**

U Hrušků (££)
Just round the corner from the Town Hall, 'At the Pear' serves a wide range of meals and drinks. It also caters happily for tour groups.
✉ **Česká 23** ☎ **(38) 731 8099**

Česky Krumlov

Krčma Markéta (££)
A period Renaissance pub within the château gardens, where chicken and game are served after being cooked over an open fire. Drinks are presented in pewter mugs and 'servants' appear wearing medieval costumes. Music is also performed.
✉ **Latrán 67** ☎ **(337) 711 453**

Pivnice Eggenberg (££)
A beer bar and restaurant in the historic Eggenberg brewery. Czech specialities are served here, and, needless to say, there is also plenty of excellent beer – light and dark – on tap.
✉ **Latrán 27** ☎ **(337) 711 426**

Restaurant Jelenka (££)
Period restaurant serving traditional Bohemian cuisine. Meals can be enjoyed on the large terrace.
✉ **Jelení zabrada** ☎ **(337) 711 283**

Karlovy Vary

Café Pizzeria Venezia (££)
The usual range of Italian specialities, served on the terrace during the summer months.
✉ **Zahradní 60** ☎ **(17) 29 721**

Promenáda (£££)
A hit with the locals, this much sought-after dining spot serves Czech specialities, international cuisine and vegetarian dishes. There is also a selection of more than 70 wines dating back to 1974. Advance reservations are recommended.
✉ **Tržiště 31** ☎ **(17) 25 648**

Kutná Hora

Piazza Navona (££)
A busy Italian restaurant and pizzeria with terrace tables, just off the main square. Multi-lingual menu. Takes all credit and debit cards.
✉ **Palackého náměsti** ☎ **(327) 512 588**

U Havířů (££)
Czech *vinarna* (wine cellar), where there is dancing as

well as eating and drinking. Medieval feasts arranged for parties.

✉ Šultysova 154
☎ (327) 513 997

U Morového Sloupu (££)
Small intimate restaurant with a pleasing garden terrace. Takes all cards.

✉ Šultysova 173
☎ (327) 513 810

Mělník

Občerstvení U Tomáše (£)
A relaxed and friendly local restaurant which offers a varied Czech menu and local wines.

✉ Náměstí Miru 30
☎ (206) 627357

U Cinků (££)
Garden restaurant offering Czech and Italian specialities, as well as a selection of fish dishes.

✉ Českolipská 1166
☎ (206) 670401

Plzeň

Na stilce (£££)
A large beer hall on the premises of the Prazdroj (Pilsner Urquell) Brewery; serving a range of Czech and international dishes – although most customers are here for the beer.

✉ Veleslavínova 6
☎ (19) 722 4955

U Salzmannů (££)
The oldest pub in town, serves Czech and international cuisine in simple but attractive surroundings with beer, naturally enough, available on tap.

✉ Pražská 8
☎ (19) 723 5484

Tábor

Atrium (££)
Located in the atrium of the new Slovan Commercial Centre, this Czech restaurant also serves a selection of Moravian wines.

✉ Slovan Centre, 9 Května
☎ (361) 251 926

U Červeného Koně (££)
If you're not put off by horse(!) on the menu – hence the name 'At the Red Horse', you'll enjoy the more conventional Czech dishes.

✉ Žižkovo náměstí
☎ (361) 470 159

U Kalicha (££)
In the historic centre of Tábor, this traditional restaurant serves Czech and international dishes.

✉ Žižkovo náměstí
☎ (361) 290 701

Třeboň

Bistro U Kapra (£)
Třeboň is famous for its carp ponds and this is as good a place as any to sample the area's fish specialities. Meat dishes also available.

✉ Dukelská 106
☎ None

Šupina Bar-Restaurant (££)
Fish specialities are served inside the restaurant, as well as on the terrace.

✉ Valy 155
☎ (333) 721149

U Čochtana (££)
Housed in historic surroundings, this wine cellar dates from the 18th century. Excellent Czech cuisine is served here.

✉ Březanova 7
☎ (333) 4740

Czech Beer
Beer has been brewed in Plzeň since the town was founded in 1295 but the Prazdrój Bresery (Pilsner Urquell) dates from 1842. Visitors to the museum, located in a Gothic malthouse, learn all about brewing technology and have a chance to see the historic lager cellars. Beer-tasting is also part of the package, and meals are served in the Na spilce restaurant.

Prague

Prices

Prices are approximate, per room per night.

£££ = over 3,000Kč
££ = 1,500–3,000Kč
£ = under1,500Kč

Europa Hotel

Originally known as the 'Archduke Stepan', the Europa Hotel was rebuilt in 1903–5 by two leading exponents of art nouveau architecture, Bedřich Bendelamayer and Alois Dryák. The façade, overlooking Wenceslas Square, is decorated with graceful sculpted figures, elaborate wrought-iron balconies and a gable with a mosaic of coloured glass by Jan Förster. The decoration of the restaurant is even more extraordinary; particularly beautiful are the bronze lamps, supported by angels with flowing robes. The hotel is now rather run down, so it's better to look at than to stay in.

Betlem Club (££)

The name is a give away – this small hotel is situated just across the street from the Bethlehem Chapel, where the religious reformer Jan Hus preached in the 15th century. Easy access to the Old Town and there are bars and restaurants on the square.

✉ **Betlémské náměstí 9, Praha 1** ☎ **2421 6872**
🚇 **Národní třída**

Bílý Lev (££)

The location of the 'White Lion' in the eastern suburb of Žižkov may be a little remote, but prices and facilities are reasonable.

✉ **Cimburkova 20, Praha 3**
☎ **271 126** 🚌 **5, 9, 26**

Corinthia Towers Hotel (£££)

This modern high-rise is fairly remote from the centre but is accessible by metro. What you pay for are the comprehensive facilities, including restaurants, shops, bars, a fitness centre and bowling alley.

✉ **Kongresová 1, Praha 4**
☎ **6119 1111** 🚇 **Vyšehrad**

Estec Hostel Strahov (£)

Reasonable access to Prague Castle is one of this hostel's advantages. Facilities include a breakfast room and bar. If Estec is booked up try the Petros and Sakbuild hostels up the road.

✉ **Vaníčkova 5/ blok 5, Praha 6**
☎ **521 250** 🚇 **Dejvická**

Hotel Adria (£££)

This completely renovated hotel near the Franciscan Gardens has excellent facilities, including satellite TV, bars, a choice of restaurants, sauna, fitness centre etc.

✉ **Václavské náměstí 26, Praha 1** ☎ **2108 1111** 🚇 **Můstek**

Hotel Bílá Labut (££)

The reasonably priced 'White Swan' boasts an excellent location on the edge of the Old Town. All 45 rooms have satellite TV and there is a night bar and restaurant.

✉ **Biskupská 9, Praha 1**
☎ **2481 1382** 🚇 **Florenc**

Hotel Hoffmeister (£££)

Prague's beautifully refurbished 'personal luxury hotel' enjoys an enviable position below the bend on the road leading up to Prague Castle.

✉ **Pod bruskou 7, Praha 1**
☎ **5101 7111; fax 5101 7100**
🚇 **Malostranská**

Hotel Intercontinental Prague (£££)

One of the city's most expensive hotels, the Intercontinental is most favoured by business travellers. The hotel has been renovated but the rooms are on the small side. Facilities include health club, jacuzzi and sauna.

✉ **Náměstí Curieových 43/5**
☎ **2488 1111**
🚇 **Staroměstská**

Hotel Nusle (££)

Good value modern hotel at the Vyšehrad end of town. Bar snacks available all day.

✉ **Závišova 30, Praha 4**
☎ **2556 2015** 🚌 **7, 18, 24**

Hotel Paříž (£££)

An eye-catching neo-Gothic building with art nouveau flourishes, the Paříž has undergone extensive restoration work and is considered to be one of the city's top hotels.

✉ **U Obecního domu 1, Praha 1**
☎ **2422 2151** 🚇 **Náměstí Republiky**

Kampa (££)

In an attractive Lesser Town location, this modernised hotel occupies a building dating from the 17th century and is popular with tour groups.

✉ **Všehradová 16, Praha 1**
☎ **2451 0408** 🚌 **12, 22**

Pension Páv (££)

Comfortable hotel located in historical old Prague. Proximity to the famous brewery, U Fleků means some rooms can be very noisy in the early evening.

✉ **Křemencova 13, Praha 1**
☎ **2491 3286** 🚇 **Národní třida**

Romantik Hotel U Raka (£)

Situated in the picturesque Nový Svět, this small pension is in great demand, so book well in advance.

✉ **Černínská 10, Praha 1**
☎ **2051 1100** 🚌 **22**

Savoy (£££)

One of Prague's leading hotels, the Savoy is only a stone's throw from Hradčany. The rooms are well appointed and there's a reassuringly unhurried ambience.

✉ **Kapelerova 6, Praha 1**
☎ **2430 2430** 🚌 **22**

U Krále Jiřího (£)

A popular pension located above two Old Town bars, this is inevitably noisy at night unless you can get one of the back rooms. All rooms are equipped with showers, telephones and televisions and there's a bar and restaurant.

✉ **Liliová 10, Praha 1**
☎ **2424 8797**
🚇 **Staroměstská**

U Tří Pštrosů (£££)

Once the centre of a flourishing trade in feathers (► panel), 'At the Three Ostriches' is a charming hostelry with a good location near the Charles Bridge. The restaurant has a deservedly good reputation.

✉ **Dražického náměstí 12, Praha 1** ☎ **2451 0779**
🚇 **Malostranská**

U Zlatých nůžek (££)

A friendly welcome is guaranteed in this hotel located in the attractive surroundings of Na Kempě. Small restaurant and bar.

✉ **Na Kempě, Praha 1**
☎ **5731 5879**

Villa Voyta (££)

A charming suburban hotel, designed as a roadside inn in 1912 by Art Nouveau architect, Josef Vojtěch. Excellent French restaurant with regularly changing menu.

✉ **K Novému dvoru 124/54, Praha 4** ☎ **472 2711**

Accommodation Agencies

Will help you find affordable accomodation. They are useful if you are looking for traditional bed and breakfast in a small hotel, guest house or pension.

Prague Bed and Breakfast Association

This well-established agency offers private and hotel accommodation in all price categories. The helpful staff speak English.

✉ **Kroftova 3, Praha 5**
☎ **5732 6897** 🚌 **6, 9, 12**

PIS (Prague Information Service)

The accommodation on offer from the Prague Information Service is mainly in pensions or private homes.

✉ **Na Příkopě 20, Praha 1**
☎ **544 444** 🚇 **Můstek**

The Three Ostriches

One of Prague's most charming hotels is the quaintly named 'At the Three Ostriches' (U Tří Pštrosů). It was built in 1606 by Jan Fux, a well-known supplier of ostrich feathers to the nobility, who used them to decorate their caps and hats. The restored interiors have preserved the original painted wooden Renaissance ceilings, together with some of the antique furniture.

Outside Prague

Finding a Room in Brno

Visitors to Brno should be aware that the demand for accommodation during Trade Fairs is high and that some hotels are frequently booked out. (Price hikes can also be expected.) If you arrive without a place to stay, your best bet is the Čedok office at Masarykovo 37, ☎ (05) 4221 0942.

Brno

Grandhotel Brno (£££)

Brno's best hotel has a prime site opposite the busy railway station. The extensive modern facilities include a nightclub, a casino and two first-class restaurants.
✉ Benešova 18–20 ☎ (5) 4232 1287

České Budějovice

Hotel U Solné Brány (££)

An attractive hotel in the quiet location of the Diocesan Gardens. Every room has a balcony and TV and there's a good restaurant.
✉ Radniční ulice 11 ☎ (38) 635 4121

Hotel U Tří Lvů (£££)

Located only a few minutes' walk from the main square, 'At the Three Lions' has facilities including its own restaurant, night club and fitness centre.
✉ U Tří Lvů 3a ☎ (38) 635 9900

Hotel Zvon (££)

Situated in the main square, this large, well-established hotel has been completely renovated and now boasts no fewer than three restaurants.
✉ Náměstí Přemysla Otakara II 28 ☎ (38) 7311 3834

Český Krumlov

Hotel Bohemia Gold (£££)

A modern, attractive hotel with restaurant and wine bar. Horse-riding can be arranged locally for guests.
✉ Plešivec 55, Městsky park ☎ (337) 712 552

Hotel Růže (££)

This stunning Renaissance building overlooking the Vltava dates from 1586–90 and once served as a hostel for members of the Jesuit Order. There are 53 rooms available, including 34 doubles and 12 Jesuit cells (double rooms without facilities for those on retreat). The hotel also has its own café and restaurant and organises sightseeing tours.
✉ Horní 154 ☎ (337) 772 100

Pension Falko (£)

All rooms in this modest hotel have shower, WC and minibar and some have satellite TV. Wheelchair access.
✉ Rooseveltova 152 ☎ (337) 716 262

Pension Na Louži (£)

Clean and centrally located pension with its original 1930s interior. Czech restaurant and beer from the barrel
✉ Kájovská 66 ☎ (337) 711 280

Karlovy Vary

Dvořák (£££)

The facilities in this top-class hotel are unrivalled, and include such luxuries as a spa treatment centre, swimming pool, sauna and gym.
✉ Nová louka 11 ☎ (17) 24145

Hotel Heluan (££)

Moderate-sized hotel with facilities including restaurant, lobby bar, nightclub, summer terrace and satellite TV in some rooms.
✉ Tržiště 41 ☎ (17) 25756

Sanatorium Bristol (£££)

A top-notch spa hotel, with an attractive central location, set in its own grounds. Classical spa therapy is available; as well as several varieties of alternative treatment, including oxygen therapy, lymphatic drainage and anti-sclerosis programme.

✉ **Sadová 19** ☎ **(17) 213 111**

Kutná Hora

Hotel Lorec (£)

There are 45 beds in this clean, modern hotel which also has its own restaurant. Food available all day.

✉ **Lorecká 57** ☎ **(327) 524 455**

Hotel U Růže (£)

A small hotel which has 26 beds available and its own restaurant.

✉ **Zámecká 52** ☎ **(327) 524 115**

Hotel U Vlašského Dvora (££)

A small hotel with good facilities including an exchange office, bar, sauna and satellite TV.

✉ **28 října 511** ☎ **(327) 514 618**

Plzeň

Hotel Slovan (££)

A large, clean, moderately priced hotel with restaurant, café and bar.

✉ **Smetanovy sady 1** ☎ **(19) 722 7256**

Tabor

Hotel Kapital (££)

Twenty-four well-appointed rooms with telephones and TV. The excellent restaurant offers Bohemian and international cuisine and is well recommended.

✉ **9 Května** ☎ **(361) 256 096**

Hotel Placat (££)

Sixty-eight all-inclusive rooms in this large, modern hotel which also accomodates a bar, restaurant and nightclub.

✉ **Třída 9 Května 2471** ☎ **(361) 252 902-4**

Hotel Relax U Drsů (££)

A large, well-appointed and modern hotel with a wine bar and cellar restaurant, fitness suite, sauna, solarium, whirlpool and aerobics room.

✉ **Varšavská 2708** ☎ **(361) 263 905**

Třeboň

Bílý Koníček (££)

Located in an attractive, castellated building which dates back to the Renaissance period, 'The White Horse' has simply decorated, clean rooms and its own restaurant and terrace.

✉ **Masarykovo náměstí 97** ☎ **(333) 721 213**

Pension Siesta (£)

A pleasant, centrally located guest house with clean rooms, an attractive terrace and charming hosts.

✉ **Hradební 26** ☎ **(333) 2324**

Zlatá Hvězda (££)

Comfortable rooms with an excellent location on the main square. Brewery tours, permits for fishing, horse-riding and cycle hire can all be arranged for guests.

✉ **Masarykovo náměstí 107** ☎ **(333) 757 111**

Private Accommodation

Staying in private accommodation is becoming an increasingly attractive option for visitors to Prague (and elsewhere in the Czech Republic). There are several agencies in the town centre and one or two have branches at the main railway station. Many apartments are in good central locations and, if you come out of season, prices are especially competitive – less than half what you might expect to pay in a hotel. Summer visitors should be sure to book in advance.

Souvenirs

Ideas for Gifts

Prague is most famous for Bohemia Crystal, and it's surprising how reasonable the prices can be. Wooden toys and puppets are not only popular with children but make nice ornaments for teenage bedrooms and around the home. On Old Town Square you'll be able to pick up jester's hats, logo T-shirts and trinkets. You will find Kafka memorabilia all over the place, but the best selection is at the exhibition in U Radnice (► 39).

Bohemia Crystal

Very convenient for visitors to the Charles Bridge, the shop's large stock of crystalware includes exquisite stained glass, painted glass, high enamel and glass souvenirs.

✉ Karlova 10 ☎ 2222 1251
🚇 Staroměstská

Celetná Crystal

A large store selling a wide range of garnets, amber, porcelain and Bohemain crystal.

✉ Celetná 15, Praha 1
☎ 232 4022 🚇 Náměstí Republiky

Česká lidová remesla

Czech folk art from easter eggs to straw nativities. Branches at Melantrichova, Mostecká and Nerudova.

✉ Jilská 22, Praha 1 ☎ 2423 2745 🚇 Můstek

Český Národní Podnik

A colourful shop specialising in traditional Czech handicrafts, especially wooden toys and ornaments and fabrics.

✉ Husova 12, Praha 1
☎ 2421 0886 🚇 Staroměstská

Crystalland

A huge modern emporium selling a wide range of Czech glassware, crystal and porcelain.

✉ Národní 15, Praha 1
☎ 2422 1158 🚇 Národní třída

Fantasy Shop

Conveniently located just off Old Town Square, Fantasy Shop is one of the capital's biggest outlets for Czech crystal.

✉ Kaprova 14, Praha 1
☎ 232 8375 🚇 Staroměstská

Havelské tržiště

This central fruit and vegetable market also has a couple of souvenir and craft stalls.

✉ Havelská, Praha 1
🚇 Můstek

Moser

A selection of superb quality porcelain and crystal for those for whom money is no object. Crystal and porcelain made in Carlsbad (Karlov Vary) and also porcelain from Meissen and Herend.

✉ Na příkopě 12, Praha 1
☎ 2421 1293 🚇 Můstek

Museum Shop Pražský Hrad

Located close to Golden Lane, the shop sells posters, cards, art books, silk ties and scarves, jewellery, glass and porcelain – much of it inspired by Prague's major monuments. An example to other souvenir shops worldwide.

✉ Purkrabství Jiřská ulice 6, Praha 1 ☎ 2437 3232 🚌 22

Old Town Square Market

Souvenirs are on sale here daily, including scarves, puppets, wooden toys and wrought-iron work made in the forge.

✉ Staroměstské náměstí, Praha 1 ☎ None
🚇 Staroměstská

Sklo Bohemia

Sklo Bohemia sells Czech crystal direct from Svá nad Sázavou in the Moravian highlands. This outlet stocks a variety of designs, which include frosted vases, coloured wine glasses and even crystal beer mugs.

✉ Na příkopě 17, Praha 1
☎ 2421 0574 🚇 Můstek

Art & Antiques

Antikvariát 'U Karlova Mostu'
A paradise for collectors of rare books, this wonderful shop specialises mostly in German and ancient Latin texts, and sells some maps.
✉ **Karlova 2, Praha 1** ☎ **2422 9205** Ⓜ **Staroměstská**

Bazar Klipy Antik
A real pot-pourri of the rare and the commonplace, from stamp collections and worn leather jackets to Biedermeier and Louis XVIII furniture.
✉ **Vyšehradská 8, Praha 2** ☎ **2491 2766** 🖷 **18 24**

Galerie Art Praha
A representative selection of some of the finest contemporary works by Czech artists, including distinguished names like Bohumír Dvorský and Karel Souček.
✉ **Staroměstské náměstí 20, Praha 1** ☎ **2421 1087** Ⓜ **Staroměstská**

Galerie České Plastiky
A gallery which focuses exclusively on post-1900 Czech sculpture, including statues and busts by the great Otto Gutfreund, Jan Hána and Emanuel Kodet.
✉ **Revoluční 20, Praha 1** ☎ **231 0684** Ⓜ **Náměstí Republiky**

Galerie Jakubská
Permanent exhibition of work by modern Czech artists, and temporary exhibitions of work by artists from Russia and elsewhere.
✉ **Jakubská 4, Praha 1** ☎ **232 7210** Ⓜ **Náměstí Republiky**

Galerie Pallas
Beautifully located in the old Ungelt courtyard, this gallery concentrates on Cubist, Expressionist and Surrealist works by such 20th-century masters as Jan Čapek, Emil Filla and Antonín Procházko.
✉ **Týn 1, Praha 1** ☎ **2489 5410** Ⓜ **Staromá**

Galerie Peithner-Lichtenfels
A small, well-established gallery dealing in works by 19th- and 20th-century Czech masters, including Otto Gutfreund, Bohumil Kubišta and Toyen (Marie Čermínová).
✉ **Michalská 12, Praha 1** ☎ **2422 7680** Ⓜ **Můstek**

Obecní dům
The museum shop in the Municipal House picks up on the Art Nouveau/Art Deco theme with novelty items including headscarves, vases, jewellery, ties, and candlesticks (► 61).
✉ **Náměstí Republiky, Praha 1** ☎ **2200 2100** Ⓜ **Náměstí Republiky**

Starožitnosti "Na Francouzské"
A small shop in Vinohrady selling rugs, porcelain statues, vases, gold and other decorative items.
✉ **Francouzská 18, Praha 2** ☎ **2424 6605** Ⓜ **Náměstí Míru** 🖷 **4 15 22 57**

U sv Heleny
Come here just to buy cigarettes, or browse among the bric-à-brac and low-value antiques.
✉ **Na poříčí 35, Praha 1** ☎ **231 7668** Ⓜ **Náměstí Republiky**

Shopping A–Z
Prague's shops are concentrated in three main areas: the honeycomb of arcades around Václavské náměstí, Národní třída and Na příkopě – a particularly useful street with tourist information, change shops and banks. For antiques, antiquarian bookshops and craft shops, try Karlova, near the Charles Bridge. Staroměstské náměstí and the neighbouring streets are useful for gifts, postcards, guide books, T-shirts, novelties etc. Pařížská is known for its boutiques and clothing stores, and the Pavilon on Vinohradská is also worth a browse.

Jewellery, Accessories & Department Stores

Czech Gem

The Czech national gemstone is the garnet, mostly mined in the vicinity of Teplica, about 50km northwest of Prague. Take note that fakes are common, so shop at the more reputable outlets, which include Ametyst zlatnictví ⊠ Vodičkova 31, Praha 1 or Dušák Zlatnictví ⊠ Na příkopě 17, Praha 1.

České Granat

Items sold at Ceské Granat include garnets, amber necklaces, bracelets and pendants. Also at Panská 1, Dlouhá 30 and Karlova 44.

⊠ **Celetná 15, Praha 1,**
☎ **267 410** 🚇 **Náměstí Republiky**

Delmas

A selection of leather goods made in the Czech Republic is sold here, including back packs and suitcases. Also some Italian leatherware.

⊠ **Vodičkova 36, Praha 1**
☎ **2423 9132** 🚇 **Můstek**
🚋 **1, 9, 14, 24, 52, 53, 55, 56**

Halada

A Czech chain which sells gold and silver, pearls, diamonds and gems, all made by the Dutch wife of the proprietor.

⊠ **Karlova 25, Praha 1**
☎ **2422 7957**
🚇 **Staroměstská**

Royal-Schubert

A range of imitation earrings, bracelets, necklaces and brooches. Alternatively, go up-market with designer jewellery by Christian Dior.

⊠ **Na příkopě 12, Praha 1**
☎ **2421 0552** 🚇 **Můstek**

Silver Shop

Attractive silver jewellery from around the world is sold in the Silver Shop, including rings with inlaid semi-precious stones.

⊠ **Železná 4, Praha 1**
☎ **2422 1991** 🚇 **Můstek**

Zlatnictví Vomáčka

Antique and second-hand jewellery and porcelain.

➕ **E4** ⊠ **Náprstkova 9, Staré Město** ☎ **2222 2017**
🚇 **Národní třída**

Department Stores

Bílá Labut'

The White Swan is a Czech-owned department store with men's and women's fashions, furniture, supermarket, florist, currency exchange, drugstore, gift shop and even its own branch of the ubiquitous US burger giant McDonalds.

⊠ **Na poříčí 23, Praha 1**
☎ **2481 1364** 🚇 **Florenc**
🚌 **24**

Kotva

Thoroughly reconstructed since the Communist era, Kotva is probably the best all-round department store in the Czech Republic. It supplies everything from designer luggage to fishing tackle.

⊠ **Náměstí Republiky 1, Praha 1** ☎ **2480 1111**
🚇 **Náměstí Republiky**

Krone

A typical European department store, with four floors and well-stocked shelves.

⊠ **Václavské náměstí 21, Praha 1** ☎ **2423 0477**
🚇 **Můstek**

Tesco

During the Communist era this was the Máj department store; then K-Mart took over. Now it is the British supermarket chain Tesco that has taken possession of the building and sells just about everything conceivable. There are good views of the city centre from the escalator.

⊠ **Národní třída 26, Praha 1**
☎ **2422 7971** 🚇 **Národní třída**
🚋 **6, 9, 18, 22, 51**

Clothing

Benetton
The famous international Italian designer offers the usual range of bright sweaters, jeans and other casual wear for both men and women.
✉ Na příkopě 4, Praha 1
☎ 2421 1225 Ⓜ Můstek

Diesel
Stylish clothes for the young and the young at heart, suitable for nightclubbing.
✉ Vodičkova 23, Praha 1
☎ 2421 6464 Ⓜ Můstek
🚋 3, 9, 14, 24, 52, 53, 55, 56

Dům Mody
The Fashion House has five floors of clothing suited to the whole family.
✉ Václavské náměstí 58
Ⓜ Muzeum

Double R
A large selection of Lee, Wrangler and other denim brands, along with other casual clothes, such as sweatshirts, jackets and cotton shirts.
✉ Karlovo náměstí 17, Praha 2
☎ 295 154 Ⓜ Karlovo náměstí

Himi's Jeans
A Czech shop, located in a recently restored turn-of-the-century shopping arcade, selling jeans, shirts, tank tops, skirts, etc at reasonable prices.
✉ Koruna palác, Václavské náměstí 1, Praha 1 ☎ 2451 1353 Ⓜ Můstek

Ivana Follová
One of the most original and creative of Czech designers, Follová produces extremely attractive dresses and blouses, many of which have been personally hand-dyed.

Shoppers also come here to buy the novelty purses.
✉ Maiselova 21, Praha 1
☎ 231 9529 Ⓜ Staroměstská

Lucerna Arcade
Vaclev Havel's grandfather designed this splendid Art Nouveau shopping arcade where you'll now find a number of fashion boutiques and occasional shows.
✉ Štěpánská 61/Vodičkova 36, Praha 1 Ⓜ Muzeum

Pavilon
This former market hall has been restored as an attractive modern shopping mall including cafés and fashion shops.
✉ Vinhradská 50, Praha 1
🚋 11

Piano Boutique
A selection of fashionable clothing from the best-known Czech designers, including Timoure et Group, Boheme and Marcela Kotěšovcová – sold here at reasonable prices.
✉ Vinohradská 47, Praha 2
☎ 379 268 Ⓜ Jiřího z Poděbrad 🚋 11

Podium
One of many fashion stores on this street, Podium features clothes by Karl Lagerfeld, Cerutti, Mayerfeld and other voguish designers.
✉ Pařížská 7, Praha 1 ☎ 232 3085 Ⓜ Staroměstská

Prostějov
A range of exceptional quality Czech-made menswear by Prostějov – worth investigating, and not too expensive.
✉ Na poříčí 14, Praha 1
☎ 2481 1393 Ⓜ Náměstí Republiky 🚋 24

Czech Them Out
'Hello Boys!' Everyone remembers Eva Herzigova and the Wonderbra advert, but now the celebrity model is no longer a lone Czech on the international catwalk. Most of the new generation of models, including Simona Krajinova and Tereza Maxova, were discovered by the thrusting owner of the Czechoslavk Models agency, Milada Karašová. Most successful to date is Daniela Peštová, currently making $12,000 a day working for L'Oreal – she already has her own page on the Internet.

Food & Drink

Ready to Eat
Several restaurants offer takeaway and/or delivery services which may come in handy, especially if you're living in private accommodation. You can pick up a grilled chicken at Grill Bono Spálená 43, Praha 1, or something healthier, including sandwiches and soups, at Cornucopia ✉ Jungmannova 10, Praha 1 ☎ 2422 7742. Food Taxi ☎ 2251 6732, operates a takeaway and delivery service, drawing on 9 restaurants and featuring Italian, Chinese and Czech dishes.

Country Life
A refuge for vegans and strict vegetarians who find themselves unable to cope with Prague's carnivorous restaurant scene. Seeds, muesli, dried food, soya products, wholewheat bread, veggie sandwiches and other items.
✉ **Melantrichova 15, Praha 1**
☎ **2421 3366**
🚇 **Staroměstská**

Cukrárna Monika
Cukrárna Monika is a small bakery which offers a beguiling selection of sweets – everything from elaborate wedding cakes to tasty ice cream sundaes.
✉ **Charvátova 11, Praha 1**
☎ **2421 1622**
🚇 **Staroměstska**

Cukrárna Simona
Small shop on Wenceslas Square, packed with sweets and chocolates. Also *Becherovka*, *Slivovice* and *Kokos* (Czech liqueurs)
✉ **Václavské náměstí 14, Praha 1** ☎ **2422 7535**
🚇 **Můstek**

Dum lahudek u Rotta
Formally a hardware store this is now one of the best delis in Prague. Choose from its vast selection of local and regional cheeses, sausages, patés, caviar and pastries.
✉ **Malé náměstí 3, Praha 1** ☎ **2423 4457** 🚇 **Staroměstská**

Fruits de France
Fruits de France changed the face of food shopping in Prague after the Velvet Revolution and stocks rarities like passion fruits and seedless grapes, as well as a varied selection of dried fruits and nuts.

✉ **Jindřišská 9, Praha 1**
☎ **2422 0304** 🚇 **Můstek**

Jan Paukert
Czech delicatessen selling Italian prosciutto, imported cheeses and other products; also well-stocked with European wines.
✉ **Národní třída 17, Praha 1**
☎ **265278** 🚇 **Národní třída**
🚊 **6, 9, 18, 22, 51**

Julius Meinl
Julius Meinl is an Austrian-owned supermarket chain and stocks a wide variety of imported cheeses, fruit and vegetables, as well as other basic goods.
✉ **Náměstí Republiky 8, Praha 1** ☎ **705 132** 🚇 **Náměstí Republiky**

Michelské Rekárny
As well as a comprehensive selection of Czech breads, this large bakery sells filled pastries, cakes, doughnuts and pancakes.
✉ **Dlouhá 1, Praha 1**

Wine Shop Ungelt
The brick-vaulted 14th-century cellar makes an atmospheric setting for the daily wine tastings, while the shop stocks quality wines from around the world.
✉ **Týnský dvůr 7, Praha 1**
☎ **2482 7501**

Zemark
Large, central grocery shop with an appetising array of salads on the delicatessen counter. Also a comprehensive choice of Moravian wines, Bohemian *Sekt*, whiskeys, liqueurs and vodkas.
✉ **Václavské náměstí 42, Praha 1** ☎ **2421 7326**
🚇 **Můstek**

Speciality Shops

Bat'a
One of the world's most famous shoe retailers, Bat'a returned to Prague after the Velvet Revolution and continues to produce foot-wear of the very highest quality.

✉ **Václavské náměstí 6, Praha 1** ☎ **2421 8133** Ⓜ **Můstek**

Capriccio
This store boasts the largest selection of sheet music in Prague: more than 10,000 items in all, including jazz and classical scores – also CDs.

✉ **Újezd 15, Praha 5** ☎ **532 507** 🚋 **12, 27, 57**

Cizojazyčné Literatura
Forgotten to pack some reading matter for the trip? Look no further than Cizojazyčné Literatura, which specialises in foreign literature in English, German, Italian and other languages. Also has a good range of guides and postcards.

✉ **Na příkopě 27 Praha 1** ☎ **262 837** Ⓜ **Můstek**

Dům Sportu
Central shop with a comprehensive range of sportwear and sporting equipment.

✉ **Jungmannova 28, Praha 1** Ⓜ **Můstek**

Kastner Ohler
This store sells a wide range of sports clothing and equipment – the ideal place if you find yourself in need of a little exercise but have forgotten to pack your tracksuit!

✉ **Václavské náměstí 66, Praha** ☎ **2422 5432** Ⓜ **Muzeum**

Knihkupectví Ma Můstku
Small, but useful bookshop selling a range of art glossies and books about Prague as well as general titles.

✉ **Na Příkopě 3, Praha 1** ☎ **2421 6383** Ⓜ **Můstek**

Knihkupectví U Černé Matky Boží
Central bookshop with a good selection of maps and guide books in English and other languages.

✉ **Celetná 34, Praha 1** ☎ **2221 1275** Ⓜ **Můstek**

Kodak Express
Camera equipment including film and batteries and a 1-hour processing service.

✉ **Branches at: Ninohradská 6; Komunardů 19 and Metro Hradčanská**

The Globe Bookstore and Coffeehouse (£)
This bookstore-cum-café is a good source for English language versions of contemporary classics by writers such as Milan Kundera and Václav Havel.

✉ **Pstrosova 6, Praha 1** ☎ **2491 6264** Ⓜ **Národní třída** 🚋 **6, 9, 17, 21, 22, 23, 51, 54, 58**

Tobacco, Cigars & Pipes
An Aladdin's cave of Cuban cigars, tobacco, cigarette-lighters and pipes.

✉ **Pavilon, Vinohradská 50, Praha 2** ☎ **2423 3125** 🚋 **11**

U Jednorožce
One of Old Town Square's most distinguished historic houses, 'At the Unicorn' sells maps, guides, comics and a good selection of postcards.

✉ **Staroměstské náměstí 17, Praha 1** ☎ **2421 0606** Ⓜ **Staroměstská**

Kafka's Store
Franz Kafka's father, Hermann, ran a haberdashery business which fascinated his young son. He was notoriously rude to staff and abrupt with customers but that didn't seem to affect his business, which prospered over the years. In 1886 the store moved from Old Town Square to larger premises in Celetná 3, then 12.

Children in Prague

Tram Rides

Prague's red-and-cream trams are a familiar sight on the streets of the town and are fascinating to children who haven't seen them operating at home. The most scenic route is No 22, which winds around the Malá Strana and Hradčany.

Activities

Club Lávka

Paddle boats are available for hire below the Charles Bridge.

✉ **Novotného Lávka 1, Praha 1**
☎ **2421 4797**
🚇 **Staroměstská**

Cruises

There is a one-hour river cruise which takes you past all the familiar city landmarks, including Prague Castle, the Charles Bridge, the National Theatre and Na Kampě. Boats set off from the jetty at Čechův most on the Na Frantisku embankment.

The Exhibition Ground

In the inner suburb of Holešovice, the extensive Exhibition Grounds have an old-fashioned fun-fair, a swimming pool and a planetarium which presents four shows daily between 2 and 5PM.

✉ **Výstaviš Praha 7, Holešovice** ☎ **827 9204**

Petřín Park

Petřín Park is a good place to head for with the children on a warm day, after a morning's sightseeing in the castle perhaps. Take a picnic lunch with you and enjoy the wonderful views, then explore the labyrinth of mirrors in the Mirror Maze and take a ride on the funicular.

Pony Traps

Take a pony trap ride from Old Town Square through Josefov (summer months only).

Tram Rides

(► panel)

Eateries

Bohemia Bagel

Filling snacks in a friendly and informal setting.

✉ **Újezd 16, Praha 1** ☎ **530 921**

Ovocné Lahůdky

Situated right in the middle of Wenceslas Square, this milk bar sells a mouth-watering selection of ice cream, milk shakes, fruit cocktails and cakes, freshly pressed juices and home-made pastries. You serve yourself and pay the bill on leaving.

✉ **Václavské náměstí 52, Praha 1** ☎ **2423 0868**
🚇 **Můstek**

U Tří Bílých Jehňátek

This is the ideal stopover if you find yourself in the vicinity of Lesser Town Square, 'At the Three White Lambs' is an old Bohemian sugar bakery tempting the sweet-toothed with such delights as *zloutkovy vénezek*, an egg ring filled with vanilla cream and topped with sugar icing, and the delicious *rakvicka*, filled with whipped or chocolate cream.

✉ **Josefská 2/44, Praha 1**
☎ **531 094** 🚇 **Malostranská**
🚊 **12, 27, 57**

Museums, Shops, Sights and Theatres

Muzeum Hraček (Toy Museum)

A treat is in store for your children at this fascinating museum set in the grounds of Prague Castle. The toy array spans 150 years and includes a fascinating collection of dolls and model

houses, cars, aircraft, paddle steamers, trains, farmyards, teddy bears and dolls, robots, musical toys and tin clockwork toys. An intriguing and enjoyable museum for adults, as well.
☒ Jiřská 6, Hradčany
☎ 2437 2294 ⏰ Daily
9:30–5:30. Closed Mon ⏹ 22

Národní Technické Muzeum (National Technical Museum)
A popular venue for Czech school parties, the Transport Hall of the museum has a wonderful collection of handsome vintage cars, old trains, motorcycles and aeroplanes. For the really adventurous visitors there is a simulated coal mine (➤ 60). There are also interesting exhibits on photography and astronomy.
☒ Kostelní 42, Praha 7
☎ 2039 9111 ⏰ Tue–Sun 9–5
☒ Vltavská ⏹ 1, 26

Shops

Albatross
An excellent stopping-off point if your children are beginning to grow restless, Albatross has an enticing selection of children's picture books, stories, fairy-tales etc.
☒ Havelská 20, Praha 1
☎ 2422 9322 ☒ Můstek

Dřevěné Hračky
The name – 'Wooden Toys' – says it all. There are pigs on wheels, elephants on wheels, train sets, mobiles and a lot more besides – and they are sold at reasonable prices.
☒ Melantrichova 17, Praha 1
☎ 2421 0886
☒ Staroměstská

Handmade
A shop specialising in home-made wooden toys and puppets.
☒ Nerudova 31, Praha 1
☒ Staroměstská

Sights

The sights of Prague are as appealing to children as they are to adults. Some of the highlights are:
The Astronomical Clock on the Old Town Hall (➤ 22)
The Gargoyles on St Vitus's Cathedral (➤ 18)
The tiny, colourfully painted houses on Golden Lane (➤ 73)

Zoologická Zahrada (Prague Zoo)
This zoo, though nothing to write home about, is more likely to entertain children than the nearby Troja Château!
☒ U Trojského zámku 3, Troja
☎ 6641 0480 ⏰ Daily 9–7
☒ Bus 112

Theatres

Národní Divadlo Marionet (National Marionette Theatre)
It's well worth investigating the programme of productions here. The theatre has matinée, as well as evening performances (➤ 112).
☒ Žatecka 1, Praha 1 ☎ 232 2536 ☒ Staroměstská

Spejbl and Hurvínek Theatre
Shows for children feature the comic character, Hurvínek (Spejbl is aimed at adults).
☒ Dejvická 38, Praha 6
☎ 312 1241

Playgrounds
After a museum or two, your children will probably be in the mood to stretch their legs and run around. There are small children's playgrounds all over town, for example on Masná (in the Jewish Quarter), and plenty of open spaces – Karlovo náměstí, to name just one.

Entertainment

Beethoven in Prague

Most visitors to Prague are
aware of the Mozart
connection, but how many
know that another great
composer, Ludwig van
Beethoven, also came
here on one occasion? The
house where the 26-year-
old musician stayed in
1796 (on the corner of
Lázeňská and Maltézské
náměstí) was then the
Golden Unicorn Hotel.
During his stay, Beethoven
also gave a recital at Count
Clam-Gallas's palace on
Husova Street.

Theatres and Concert Halls

Černé Divadlo Animato (Black Light Theatre)

Pantomime with
luminescent actors and
props, performing under
black lights. The
programmes are based on
well-known stories: *Don
Quijote, Alice in Wonderland,*
Czech fairy-tales etc.
Performances begin at 8PM
and take place at several
different venues.

⊠ **Národní třída 4** ☎ **2491
4129** ⦿ **Narodní třída**

Divadlo Celetné

⊠ **Celetná 17, Praha 1** ☎
2481 2762 ⦿ **Staroměstská**

Image Theatre

⊠ **Pařížská 4, Praha 1** ☎ **231
4448** ⦿ **Staroměstská**

Ta Fantastika

⊠ **Karlova 8, Praha 1** ☎ **2222
1367** ⦿ **Staroměstská**

Divadlo Spirála

Theatre, set in the exhibition
grounds, used for popular
musicals such as *Jesus
Christ Superstar, Hair* etc.

⊠ **Výstavišt Praha 7,
Holešovice** ☎ **2010 3380**
⦿ **Nádraží Holešovice** ⦿ **5,
12, 17**

Hudební Divadlo Karlín, Karlin Musical Theatre

Standard musicals such as
Hello, Dolly! and *My Fair
Lady* produced here; also
operetta.

⊠ **Křižíkova 10, Praha 8**
☎ **2186 8149** ⦿ **Florenc**

Kongresové Centrum Praha (Congress Centre Prague)

A venue for classical
concerts, musicals and
similar productions.

⊠ **Ulice 5 května 65, Praha 4**
☎ **643 2868** ⦿ **Vyšehrad**

Laterna Magika, Magic Lantern

A multi-media show,
combining live theatre, film
and dance – not as
revolutionary a concept as
it once was, but still popular.
Performances at 5PM and
8PM.

⊠ **Národní třída 4, Praha 1**
☎ **2491 4129** ⦿ **Národní třída**
⦿ **6, 9, 18, 22, 51**

Národní Divadlo (National Theatre)

Czech National Opera
performs the mainstream
classical repertoire: Mozart,
Verdi, Puccini, Smetana *et al.*
The National Ballet Company
also performs here.
Performances usually start at
7PM. (► 59)

⊠ **Národní třída 2, Praha 1**
☎ **2492 1528** ⦿ **Národní třída**
⦿ **6, 9, 18, 22, 51**

Národní Divadlo Marionet (National Marionette Theatre)

Puppets and costumed
actors perform classical
operas like Mozart's *Don
Giovanni* as well as some
lighter fare, such as the
Beatles' *Yellow Submarine.*
Performances usually begin
at 8PM.

⊠ **Žatecka 1, Praha 1** ☎ **232
2536** ⦿ **Staroměstská**

Opera Mozart

A selection of popular arias
from Mozart operas, which
are sung here in German and
Italian.

⊠ **Novotného lávka 1, Praha 1**
☎ **232 2536** ⦿ **Staroměstská**

Rudolfinum

The city's premier concert
venue is home to the Czech
Philharmonic Orchestra, the
country's best ensemble.

WHERE TO BE ENTERTAINED

Two other excellent orchestras, the Prague Symphony and the Prague Radio Symphony also perform here. Performances begin at 7:30PM.

✉ **Náměstí Jana Palacha, Praha 1** ☎ **2489 3352**
🚇 **Staroměstská**

Smetanova síň (Smetana Hall)

Recently re-opened after an extensive restoration programme, this is a venue for symphony concerts.

✉ **Obecní dům, Náměstí Republiky 5, Praha 1** ☎ **2200 2336** 🚇 **Náměstí Republiky**

Státní Opera Praha (State Opera House)

An offshoot of the National Opera Company, this troupe concentrates on the mainstream standards, virtually to the exclusion of everything else.
Performances usually begin at 7PM.

✉ **Wilsonova 4, Praha 2**
☎ **265 353** 🚇 **Muzeum**

Stavovské Divadlo (Estates Theatre)

Mozart is performed here on a regular basis, of course, but there are also other productions, notably classical drama and occasionally ballet. Performances usually begin at 7PM.

✉ **Ovocny trh, Praha 1**
☎ **2492 1528** 🚇 **Můstek**

Cinemas

There are cinemas all over Prague, with a concentration around Wenceslas Square. Most mainstream foreign films are shown with Czech subtitles. It is best to check listings magazines for show times, but there are usually performances at around 2:30, 5 and 7:15–8. Art films are sometimes shown at the Veletržní Palác. Below is a selection of the city's cinemas:

Areo
✉ **Biskupova 31, Praha 3**
☎ **7177 1349**
🚋 **1, 9, 18, 58**

Blaník
✉ **Václavské náměstí 56, Praha 1**
☎ **2221 0110**
🚇 **Muzeum**

Broadway
✉ **Rytířská 31, Praha 1**
☎ **2161 0162**
🚇 **Můstek**

Hvězda
✉ **Václavské náměstí 38, Praha 1**
☎ **2421 6822**
🚇 **Muzeum**

Illusion
✉ **Vinohradská 48, Praha 2**
☎ **250 260**
🚇 **Jiřího z Podebrad**

Kotva
✉ **Náměstí Republiky 8, Praha 1** ☎ **2481 1482**
🚇 **Náměstí Republiky**

MAT Studio
✉ **Karlovo náměstí 19, Praha 1**
☎ **2491 5765**
🚇 **Karlovo náměstí**

Perštýn
✉ **Na Perštýné 6**
☎ **2166 8432**
🚇 **Národní třída**

U Hradeb
✉ **Mostecká 21, Praha 1**
☎ **535 006**
🚇 **Malostranská**

Tinsel Town

Prague has been playing host to Western film-makers ever since Miloš Forman arrived to make Amadeus in 1984. Recently more and more foreign directors have been heading for the Czech capital, which offers locations of unrivalled beauty, highly trained, home-grown film technicians and the largest studios in the region. Fortunately the income is proving hugely beneficial to the Czech film industry, now wholly reliant on private funding.

Discos, Clubs & Bars

Ticket Offices
To get hold of tickets for the theatre or other events, try one of the city's central ticket offices: **Bohemia Ticket International** Na Příkopé 16, Praha 1 ☎ 2421 5031; **Top Theatre Tickets** ✉ Celetná 13, Praha 1 ☎ 232 2536, or TicketPro ✉ Salvátorská 10, Praha 1 ☎ 2481 4020

Discos and Clubs

AghaRTA Jazz Centrum
Local and international jazz bands perform here. There's a jazz shop on site too, which is open Mon–Fri 5PM–midnight and Sat–Sun 7PM–midnight.
✉ **Krakovská 5, Praha 1**
☎ **2221 1275** 🕔 **Daily 9–12**
🚇 **Muzeum**

Bílý Koníček
Set in the incongruous surroundings of a 12th-century cellar, this club offers mainstream disco sounds to a young Czech crowd.
✉ **Staroměstské náměstí 20, Praha 1** ☎ **2422 0947** 🕔 **Daily 8PM–5AM** 🚇 **Staroměstská**

Casino Hotel Ambassador
The usual selection of casino activities is offered here, including roulette, black jack, punto banco, poker, craps and slot machines.
✉ **Václavské náměstí 5-7, Praha 1** ☎ **2419 3681** 🕔 **Daily 24 hours** 🚇 **Můstek**

Club Lávka
Virtually everything is going on in this attractive building with its own located, below the Charles Bridge: theatre, coffee room, jazz parties – even fashion shows.
✉ **Novotného Lávka 1, Praha 1** ☎ **2421 4797** 🕔 **Daily 24hours. Disco daily 10PM** 🚇 **Staroměstská**

Jazz Club Železná
A reliable, mainstream jazz club in the heart of the Old Town.
✉ **Železná 16, Praha 1** ☎ **2423 9697** 🚇 **Můstek**

Karlovy lázně
Four clubs in one – playing a variety of music including rock standards, golden oldies and dance.
✉ **Novotného lávka, Praha 1** ☎ **2421 4797** 🕔 **Daily until late** 🚊 **17, 18**

Klub Lavka
This vast entertainments complex on the Vltava has a riverside terrace where you can enjoy a drink from the cocktail bar, where tequilas are a speciality. Other attractions include indoor and outdoor dining spaces, a theatre, dance floors and an internet café.
✉ **Novotného lavka 1, Praha 1** ☎ **2421 4797** 🚊 **17, 18**

Lucerna Music Bar
A popular traditional venue, which specialises in Czech pop, Beatles and Rolling Stones revivals and covers bands.
✉ **Vodičkova 36, Praha 1** ☎ **2421 7108** 🕔 **Daily 7PM–6AM, concerts at 9PM** 🚇 **Můstek** 🚊 **3, 9, 14, 24, 52, 53, 55, 56**

Red Hot & Blues
Jazz and blues club with live bands every night. Also has a popular Tex-Mex-style restaurant with courtyard seating when the weather is favourable (➤ 95).
✉ **Jakubska 12, Praha 1** ☎ **231 4639**

Reduta Jazz Club and Rock Café
Swing, traditional, Dixieland and many other varieties of jazz, played by Czech bands.
✉ **Národní třída 20, Praha 1** ☎ **2491 2246** 🕔 **Daily 9PM (concerts)** 🚇 **Národní třída** 🚊 **6, 9, 18, 22, 51**

Roxy

This popular Josefov club attracts a loyal clientele that appreciates its run-down look and relaxed atmosphere.

✉ Dlouhá 33, Praha 1
☎ 2481 0951 🕓 Daily
5PM–2:30AM 🚇 Staroměstská

U Staré Paní

'At the Old Lady' is a hotel, restaurant and jazz club with live bands.

✉ Michalská 9, Praha 1
☎ 267 267 🕓 Daily 4PM–4AM
🚇 Staroměstská

Variete Praha

Come here for the usual variety of glamorous dancers, acrobats, jugglers and music.

✉ Vodvičkova 30, Praha 1
☎ 2421 5945 🕓 Daily
7:30PM–2AM. Shows
9:30PM–11:30PM 🚇 Můstek
🚌 3, 9, 14, 22, 52, 53, 55, 56

Bars

Banana Café

Situated in the same building as La Provence restaurant, this is one of Prague's trendiest establishments. DJs and occasional live shows.

✉ Štupartská 9, Praha 1
☎ 2481 6695
🚇 Staroměstská

Chapeau Rouge

Open until 5AM, this bar is almost always full to the brim and always lively. Loud music.

✉ Jakubská 2, Praha 1
☎ None 🚇 Staroměstská

Hop Store

You'll find this micro-brewery opposite the Estates Theatre. The home brew is highly-palatable, alternatively, there's a huge array of bottled beers on offer as well as salads and sandwiches.

✉ Ovocný trh, Praha 1
☎ 2423 4794

Radegast Pub

Located just off Celetná, this pleasant pub serves a variety of light and dark beers, and also has a range of bar meals.

✉ Templová 2, Praha 1
☎ 232 8069 🚇 Staroměstská

U Dvou Koček

Pilsner Urquell and live music nightly are the attractions of this traditional Czech pub.

✉ Uhelný trh 10, Praha 1
☎ 2422 9982

U Fleků

Founded in 1499, this famous historic pub serves a unique dark beer of the same name. You can drink it indoors or in the huge beer garden.

✉ Křemencova 11, Praha 1
☎ 2491 5118 🚇 Karlovo náměstí

U Medviku

A traditional pub selling Budvar beer and light meals. The garden is open in summer.

✉ Na Perštýně 7, Praha 1
☎ 2422 0930 🚇 Národní třída

U Zlatého Tygra

The beer sold in this most traditional of pubs comes direct from the 13th-century cellars. Václav Havel brought the US President Bill Clinton here when he visited Prague in 1994 (► panel).

✉ Husova 17, Praha 1
☎ 2422 9020 🚇 Můstek

U Zlatého Tygra

The no-frills beer hall is usually packed with Prague die-hards addicted to the golden nectar. To find a seat say *Je tu volno?* (Is this space free?) and wait to be served. Pilsner Urquell is the only beer available, delivered uniformly in half-litre measures. Each glass is marked on your tab and you can also order traditional Czech snacks like Prague ham with horseradish sauce. When you're ready to go, say *Platit prosím* – don't expect an itemised bill, you won't be overcharged.

What's on When

Smaller Venues
Many of Prague's palaces
and historic churches are
used for concerts,
especially in the summer.
These events are not only
enjoyable in themselves
but also allow visitors to
see some splendid
interiors not otherwise
open to the public. Some
venues to look out for are:
the Chapel of Mirrors in
the Klementinum, the
Nostitz Palace,
Lichtenstein Palace,
Lobkowicz Palace, Clam-
Gallas Palace, Bertramka,
Bethlehem Chapel, St
Agnes's Convent, St
George's Basilica and the
House at the Stone Bell.

19 January
*Anniversary of the death of
Jan Palach:*
The suicide of the young
student protester in 1968, in
protest at the Soviet invasion
of Czechoslovakia, is
commemorated at his
memorial on Wenceslas
Square and at Olšany
Cemetery.

March
International Music Festival:
A series of classical and
contemporary concerts is
performed in venues all over
the city throughout the
month.

30 April
Witches' Night:
A bonfire held on Petřín Hill
celebrates the traditional end
of winter and the birth of
spring.

Early May
Prague Spring:
A three-week programme of
classical music and dance,
performed in churches,
palaces and concert halls
around Prague. The celebrations begin with a procession
from Smetana's grave in
Vyšehrad to his namesake
concert hall in Obecní Dům,
where a celebratory performance of Ma Vlast is given.

June
Dance Prague:
An international festival of
modern dance with a variety
of events held at indoor and
outdoor venues throughout
the city.

August
International Table Tennis
Tournament.

September
Prague Autumn:
A two-week music festival is
led by the city's orchestras
and internationally renowned
soloists.

October
Mozart in Prague:
A month-long music festival
commemorating the
composer's visit to the city
in 1787.

17 November
*Anniversary of the Velvet
Revolution:*
A commemoration and
wreath-laying ceremony
conducted on Wenceslas
Square and Národní
(although there has been
much concern voiced by
citizens recently about the
poor attendance at this
event).

December
*Christmas market on Old
Town Square:*
Throughout the festive
season a giant Christmas
tree lights up the centre of
the square, while the space
around it is crammed with
market stalls selling carved
toys, bobbin lace, ceramics,
glass figurines, Christmas
ornaments and tasty ginger-
bread cakes, barbecued
sausages and mulled wine.
Entertainment is provided by
musicians, dancers, jugglers
and other performers.

Practical Matters

Above: *new banknote*
Right: *Prague telephone*

TIME DIFFERENCES

GMT
12 noon

Prague
1PM

Germany
1PM

USA (NY)
7AM

Netherlands
1PM

Spain
1PM

BEFORE YOU GO

WHAT YOU NEED

- ● Required
- ○ Suggested
- ▲ Not required

	UK	Germany	USA	Netherlands	Spain
Passport/National Identity Card	●	●	●	●	●
Visa	▲	▲	▲	▲	▲
Onward or Return Ticket	▲	▲	▲	▲	▲
Health Inoculations	▲	▲	▲	▲	▲
Health Documentation (➤ 123, Health)	●	●	▲	●	●
Travel Insurance	○	○	○	○	○
Driving Licence (national)	●	●	●	●	●
Car Insurance Certificate	●	●	●	●	●
Car Registration Document	●	●	●	●	●

WHEN TO GO

Prague

 High season

⬭ Low season

-1°C	0°C	4°C	9°C	14°C	17°C	19°C	18°C	14°C	9°C	4°C	0°C
JAN	FEB	MAR	APR	MAY	JUN	JUL	AUG	SEP	OCT	NOV	DEC

🌧 Wet   ☁ Cloud   ☀ Sun   🌦 Sunshine & showers

TOURIST OFFICES

In the UK
Czech Tourist Authority,
The Czech Centre,
95 Great Portland Street,
London W1N 5RA
☎ 020 7291 9920
Fax: 020 7436 8300

In the USA
Czech Tourist Authority,
1109–1111 Madison Avenue,
New York
NY 10028
☎ 212/288 0830
Fax: 212/288 0971

POLICE 158

AMBULANCE 155

FIRE 150

WHEN YOU ARE THERE

ARRIVING

Czechoslovak Airlines – ČSA (☎ 24 10 41 11) operates direct scheduled flights to Prague from Britain, mainland Europe and North America. Flight time from London is two hours. Prague is connected by rail to all main European capitals (➤ 121, Public Transport).

Praha Ruzyně Airport Kilometres to city centre	**Journey times**	
● **20 kilometres** ➤	🚌	40 minutes
	🚐	35 minutes
	🚗	20–25 minutes

Praha Hlavní Station In city centre	**Journey times**	
● ➤	🚌	on metro line C
	🚐	available
	🚗	available

MONEY

The monetary unit of the Czech Republic is the Koruna česká (Kč) – or Czech crown – which is divided into 100 haléř (h) – or heller – though you will not find many of the latter in Prague. There are coins of 10, 20 and 50 hellers and 1, 2, 5, 10, 20 and 50 crowns. Banknotes come in 20, 50, 100, 200, 500, 1,000 and 5,000 crowns. Money may be changed at the airport, in banks (➤ 120, Opening Hours), major hotels, Čedok offices, and in the centre of Prague at exchange offices. It is an offence to change money through street black-market money dealers; in any case, they rarely offer an attractive rate.

TIME

The Czech Republic is on Central European Time (GMT+1), but from late March, when clocks are put forward one hour, until late October, Czech Summer Time (GMT+2) operates.

CUSTOMS

 YES

Duty Free Limits:
Alcohol – spirits: 1L *and* wine: 2L
Cigarettes: 200 *or*
Cigarillos: 100 *or*
Cigars: 50 *or*
Tobacco: 250gms *or* a proportionate combination of the above tobacco products.
You must be 18 and over to benefit from the alcohol and tobacco allowance.
Perfume: 50ml *or*
Toilet water: 250ml
Gifts: not in excess of 3,000Kč per person.
Fuel: 10L in a spare can (for personal use).

 NO

Drugs, firearms, ammunition, offensive weapons, obscene material, unlicensed animals.

CONSULTATES

UK
☎ 24 51 04 39

Germany
☎ 24 51 03 23

USA
☎ 24 51 08 47

Netherlands
☎ 24 51 01 89

Spain
☎ 24 31 14 41

WHEN YOU ARE THERE

TOURIST OFFICES

**Czech Tourist Authority
(Česká centrála cestovního ruchu)**
● Národní třída 37
110 01 Praha 1
☎ /Fax: 2421 1458

**Prague Information Service
(Pražská informační služba PIS)**
● Na příkopě 20
Nové Město, Praha 1
☎ 264 022 or 544 444
Metro: Můstek or Náměstí Republiky
Open: 9AM–7PM (5PM week-ends); longer in summer

● Praha hlavní nádraží
(Main Railway Station)
Wilsonova
Praha 1
☎ 2422 4200
Metro: Hlavní nádraží
Open: 3:30AM–1AM

● Staroměstská radnice
(Old Town Hall)
Staroměstské náměstí 22
Praha 1
☎ 2448 2751
Metro: Staroměstská
Open: 9AM–6PM (closed Mon)

Prague Tourist Centre
● Rytířská 12
Nové Město
☎ 2421 2209
Metro: Můstek
Open: 9AM–8PM daily

● Karlův most
(Charles Bridge – Lesser Side Tower), Praha 1
Metro: Malostranská
Open: 10AM–6PM summer only

NATIONAL HOLIDAYS

J	F	M	A	M	J	J	A	S	O	N	D
1		(1)	(1)	2		2			1		3

1 Jan	New Year's Day
Mar/Apr	Easter Monday
1 May	May Day
8 May	Liberation Day
5 Jul	St Cyril and St Method Day
6 Jul	Jan Hus Day
28 Oct	Independence Day
24 Dec	Christmas Eve
25 Dec	Christmas Day
26 Dec	St Stephen's Day

On these days banks, offices, department stores and some shops close. However, restaurants, museums and other tourist attractions tend to stay open.

OPENING HOURS

○ Shops   ● Castles/chateaux
● Offices   ● Museums
● Banks   ● Pharmacies

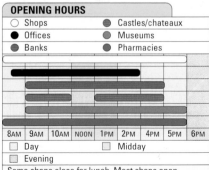

	8AM	9AM	10AM	NOON	1PM	2PM	4PM	5PM	6PM

☐ Day   ☐ Midday
☐ Evening

Some shops close for lunch. Most shops open Saturday until 12 noon or 1PM. Food shops open from 7AM; department stores and large shopping centres open until 8PM (4PM Saturday); gift shops generally 10AM–10PM. Outside Prague centre, shops close on Sunday. Some pharmacies open 24 hours. Banks vary, some open Saturday morning. Museums and art galleries usually open from 9/10AM to 5/6PM; they are closed Mondays. Castles, chateaux and other historical monuments open daily (except Monday) May to September and weekends in April and October, but may be closed other times; please check.

DRIVE ON THE
RIGHT

TOILETS
CHARGE

PUBLIC TRANSPORT

Internal Flights Czechoslovak Airlines (ČSA), Revoluční 1, Praha 1 (☎ 231 7395), and a variety of other carriers link Prague with Brno and Ostrava. Though not cheap, especially when compared with the train or bus, they are useful when you want to get somewhere quickly.

Trains Czech Railways (Československé Stání Dráhy, ČSD, ☎ 236 4441 or 264 930) run *rychlík* which stop only at major towns and *osobní* calling at every station. Services to north and east Bohemia depart from Masarykovo nádraží; routes to the south are from Smíchovské nádraží.

River Boats From April to September cruise boats chug up and down the Vltava River, as far as Troja Château in the north of Prague and Slapy Lake in the south. The Prague Steamship Company (Pražská paroplavební služba, ☎ 298 309) is the main operator. Most tours start from Paroplavební pier.

Metro Prague's metro is clean, fast and cheap. There are three lines: A (green), B (yellow), C (red). Trains run 5AM to 12 midnight, every 2 minutes peak times (5 to 10 minutes other times). The letter 'M' with a downward arrow marks a station entrance. For information (also trams and buses) ☎ 2422 5135.

Trams/Buses After the metro, trams (*tramvaje*) are the fastest way of getting around Prague. There are 23 lines running every 6 to 8 minutes peak times (10 to 15 minutes other times). Buses (*autobusy*) are of little use as they mainly keep out of the centre. There is one ticket for the metro, tram and bus.

CAR RENTAL

A car is not really necessary for Prague as much of the city centre is pedestrianised. Car rental is, however, easy to arrange but can be quite expensive. Shop around, many small local firms charge less than well known names. Esocar (☎ 278 888) is cheaper than most.

TAXIS

Taxis abound in Prague. An unoccupied taxi has a lit-up sign and may be hailed on the street or hired from a taxi rank. Registered taxis should have a meter clearly displayed. Beware of unscrupulous drivers who charge tourists what they feel like.

DRIVING

Speed limit on motorways (annual toll payable): **110kph**. Minimum limit: **50kph**

Speed limit on country roads: **90kph** (on level crossings: **30kph**)

Speed limit on urban roads: **60kph**

Must be worn in front seats – and rear seats where fitted. Under 12s may not travel in the front seat.

Don't drink *any* alcohol if driving. The allowed blood/alcohol level is zero and penalties are severe.

Petrol (*benzín*) is sold in leaded form as *special* (91 octane) and super (96 octane). Unleaded petrol comes as *natural* (95 octane) and *super plus* (98 octane), the latter is available only at larger petrol stations. Diesel (*nafta*) is also available. In Prague, filling stations are few and far between, but some open 24 hours.

ÚAMK, the Czech automobile club, operates a 24-hour nationwide breakdown service on the same terms as your own motoring club at home (non-members pay in full), ☎ 0123 (123 in Prague) or 154 from mobile phones. On motorways use emergency phones (every 2km) to summon help.

PERSONAL SAFETY

Prague is a comparatively safe city, though petty crime is on the increase, especially around Wenceslas Square, Old Town Square, Charles Bridge and the Castle. Report any loss or theft to the *Městská policie* (municipal police) – black uniforms.

- Watch your bag in tourist areas, on the metro/trams.
- Never leave anything of value on show in your car.
- Deposit your passport and valuables in the hotel safe.
- Avoid walking alone in dark alleys at night.

Police assistance:
☎ **158**
from any call box

TELEPHONES

There are public telephones on the street and near metro stations. Older orange phones, accepting only 1Kč coins, are solely for local calls. Grey phones take 1, 2, 5 and 10Kč coins. In Prague there are an increasing number of phonecard (*Telefonní karta*) booths. Buy cards for 100, 190 and 280Kč from post offices, tobacconists and newsagents. The code for Prague is 02.

International Dialling Codes

From Czech Republic to:	
UK:	00 44
Germany:	00 49
USA:	00 1
Netherlands:	00 31
Spain:	00 34

POST

Post Offices
Post Offices have distinctive orange *Pošta* signs outside. The main post office at Jindřišská 14, Nové Město is open 24 hours. There are several branches in the city which are open 8AM–7PM (12 noon Sat) and closed Sun.
☎ 2422 8856.

ELECTRICITY

The power supply in the Czech Republic is 220 volts.

Plugs are of the two-round-pin variety, so an adaptor is needed for most non-Continental European appliances and a voltage transformer for appliances operating on 100–120 volts.

TIPS/GRATUITIES

Yes ✓ No ✗		
Hotels	✗	
Restaurants	✓	10%
Cafés	✓	10%
Taxis	✓	10%
Tour guides	✓	(20Kč)
Porters	✓	(40Kč)
Usherettes	✗	
Hairdressers	✓	10%
Cloakroom attendants	✓	(2Kč)
Toilets	✓	(2Kč)

PHOTOGRAPHY

What to photograph: after years of secret police lurking on every street corner you are now free to photograph almost anywhere.
Where to buy film: Staré Město (Old Town) and Malá Strana (Lesser Quarter) have numerous small shops selling Western film. Avoid Czech colour film as you may not be able to get it processed outside the country.
Where to get film developed: photo shops are all over the tourist areas so finding a place to get your photos developed should not be a problem.

HEALTH

Insurance
Emergency medical treatment is free to foreign visitors to the Czech Republic. Nationals of EU countries are entitled to additional medical care (show passport). Private medical insurance is advised (essential for all other visitors).

Dental Services
Dental treatment must be paid for. If you require urgent treatment there is an Emergency Dental Crisis Helpline (☎ 1097). První pomoc zubní, Vladislavova 22, Nové Město (☎ 2422 7663) is open 7AM–7PM (24 hours weekends).

Sun Advice
The sun is not a real problem in Prague. June to August is the sunniest (and hottest) period but there are often thundery showers to cool things down. If the summer sun is fierce, apply a sunscreen and wear a hat, or visit a museum.

Drugs
Pharmacies (*lékárnat* or *apothéka*) are the only places to sell over-the-counter medicines. They also dispense many drugs (*leky*) normally available only on prescription in other Western countries.

Safe Water
It is not advisable to drink tap water as it is loaded with toxins and is heavily chlorinated. Bottled water is available everywhere. The still table water (*Stolní pitní voda*) is the most common.

CONCESSIONS

Students/Youths Holders of an International Identity Card (ISIC) are entitled to a 50 per cent reduction on admission to Prague's museums and galleries. Student cards also offer reductions on international trains, though not on domestic public transport. The ČKM (Czech Youth Travel Agency), Žitna 12, Praha 2 (☎ 299 454), specialises in cheap travel for young people and students in and outside the Czech Republic. Its branch at Jindřišská 28, Praha 1 (☎ 2423 0218) issues ISICs.

Senior Citizens There are no special concessions for senior citizens. However, Saga, who organise holidays for over 50s, have trips to Prague. Contact: Saga Holidays, Saga Building, Middelburg Square, Folkestone, Kent CT20 1AZ, UK (☎ 0800 414383).

CLOTHING SIZES

Czech Republic	UK	Rest of Europe	USA	
46	36	46	36	**Suits**
48	38	48	38	
50	40	50	40	
52	42	52	42	
54	44	54	44	
56	46	56	46	
41	7	41	8	**Shoes**
42	7.5	42	8.5	
43	8.5	43	9.5	
44	9.5	44	10.5	
45	10.5	45	11.5	
46	11	46	12	
37	14.5	37	14.5	**Shirts**
38	15	38	15	
39/40	15.5	39/40	15.5	
41	16	41	16	
42	16.5	42	16.5	
43	17	43	17	
34	8	34	6	**Dresses**
36	10	36	8	
38	12	38	10	
40	14	40	12	
42	16	42	14	
44	18	44	16	
38	4.5	38	6	**Shoes**
38	5	38	6.5	
39	5.5	39	7	
39	6	39	7.5	
40	6.5	40	8	
41	7	41	8.5	

- Contact the airline at least 72 hours before departure to reconfirm your booking to prevent being 'bumped' from that plane because of over-allocation.
- There is an airport departure tax which is normally included in the cost of the ticket.
- Antiques can only be exported with a certificate, issued by the National Museum or National Gallery, indicating the object is not of Czech national heritage.

LANGUAGE

The official language of the Czech Republic is Czech (Český) – a highly complex western Slav tongue. Czech sounds and looks daunting, but apart from a few special letters, each letter and syllable is pronounced as it is written – the key is always to stress the first syllable of a word.
Any attempt to speak Czech will be heartily appreciated although English is spoken by many involved in the tourist trade. Below are a few Czech words that may be helpful.

hotel	*hotel*	toilet	*záchod/WC*
room	*pokoj*	bath	*koupelnoou*
I would like a room	*potřebuji pokoje*	shower	*sprcha*
... single/double	*... jednolůžjový/ dvoulůžkový*	cold/hot water	*studená/teplá voda*
... for one night	*... na jednu noc*	towel	*ručník*
how much per night?	*kolik stojí jedna noc?*	soap	*mýdlo*
		room number	*cislo pokoje*
reservation	*reservaci*	key	*klíč*
breakfast	*snídaně*		

bank	*banku*	cheap	*levný*
post office	*pošta*	expensive	*drahý*
foreign exchange	*směnárna*	free (no charge)	*zdarma*
Czech crown	*koruna česká (kč)*	more	*více*
heller	*haléř*	less	*méně*
credit card	*credit card*	the bill	*účet*
how much?	*kolik?*	it's a rip off!	*to je zlodějina!*

restaurant	*restaurace*	lunch	*oběd*
coffee house	*kavárna*	dinner	*večeře*
pub	*hospoda*	starter	*předkrm*
wine bar	*vinárna*	main course	*hlavní jídlo*
table	*stůl*	dish of the day	*nabídka dne*
menu	*jídelní lístek*	dessert	*moučnik*
fixed-price menu	*standardní menu*	waiter	*čišník*
wine list	*nápojový lístek*	waitress	*servírka*

aeroplane	*letadlo*	pleasure steamer	*parník*
airport	*letiště*	small boat	*lodička*
train	*vlak*	ticket	*lístek*
train station	*nádraží*	... single/return	*jednosměrnou/ zpáteční*
metro station	*stanice*		
bus	*autobus*	... first/second class	*první/druhou třídu*
bus station	*autobusové nádraží*	ticket office	*pokladna*
tram	*tramvaj*	seat reservation	*místenka*
bus/tram stop	*zastávka*		

yes	*ano*	excuse me	*promiňte*
no	*ne*	sorry	*pardon*
please	*prosím*	help!	*pomoc!*
thank you	*děkuji*	today	*dnes*
hello	*ahoj*	yesterday	*včera*
goodbye	*na shledanou*	tomorrow	*zítra*
good morning	*dobré ráno*	open	*otevřeno*
goodnight	*dobrou noc*	closed	*zavřeno*

Acknowledgements
The Automobile Association wishes to thank the following photographers, libraries, associations and museums for their assistance in the preparation of this book: MARY EVANS PICTURE LIBRARY 10; MRI BANKERS' GUIDE TO FOREIGN CURRENCY 119; ROBERT HARDING PICTURE LIBRARY 89; HULTON GETTY 14; NATIONAL GALLERY OF PRAGUE 26
The remaining photographs are held in the Association's own library (AA PHOTO LIBRARY) with contributions from: C SAWYER front cover (b), front cover (c), back cover, 2, 5a, 5b, 13, 17, 18, 21, 20/1, 22, 25, 27, 31, 33, 35, 38, 46, 49, 54, 57, 60a, 60b, 64, 66b, 68, 70, 73a, 73b, 74, 75, 85; A SOUTER 1, 15b, 16, 24, 41, 44, 47, 52, 61, 62, 63a, 72; J WYAND front cover (a), front cover (d), 6a, 7, 8, 9, 11, 12, 12/3, 15a, 19, 27b, 28, 29, 32, 34, 36, 37a, 37b, 39a, 39b, 42, 43, 45, 48, 50, 51, 55a, 55b, 56, 58, 59, 65, 66a, 67, 69, 71, 77, 78, 78/9, 79, 80, 81, 82, 83, 84, 86, 87a, 87b, 88, 90, 91a, 91b, 117a, 117b, 122a, 122b, 122c

Authors' Acknowledgements
The authors would like to thank the AVE Travel Agency, the Prague Information Service (PIS), the National Gallery in Prague, and the Information offices in Český Krumlov, Kutná Hora, Plzeň, Tábor and Třeboň for their assistance with this book.

Contributors: Copy editor: Nia Williams Page Layout: The Company of Designers
Verifier: Teresa Fisher Researcher (Practical Matters): Colin Follett Indexer: Marie Lorimer
Revision management: Outcrop Publishing Services, Cumbria